FATHERS & MOTHERS

Five Papers on the Archetypal Background of Family Psychology

JAMES HILLMAN

ERICH NEUMANN

MURRAY STEIN

AUGUSTO VITALE

VERA VON DER HEYDT

SPRING PUBLICATIONS

THOMPSON, CONN.

Published by Spring Publications
Thompson, Conn.
www.springpublications.com

Third, revised edition 2025 (3.0)
First published in 1973

Cover image:
Marble grave stele with a family group, c. 360 BCE
The Metropolitan Museum of Art, New York
Rogers Fund, 1911

Library of Congress Control Number: 2025935255

ISBN 978-0-88214-185-5 (softcover)   ISBN 978-0-88214-186-2 (ebook)

CONTENTS

ABBREVIATIONS

CW = *Collected Works of C. G. Jung*, edited and translated by Gerhard Adler and
R.F.C. Hull, 20 vols. (Princeton, N.J.: Princeton University Press, 1953–79)

SE = *The Standard Edition of the Complete Psychological Works of Sigmund Freud*,
translated by James Strachey, 24 vols. (London: The Hogarth Press and
The Institute of Psycho-Analysis, 1953–73

UE = *Uniform Edition of the Writings of James Hillman*, edited by Klaus Ottmann,
12 vols. (Putnam and Thompson, Conn.: Spring Publications, 2004–)

The Great Mother, Her Son, Her Hero, and the Puer

JAMES HILLMAN

Perhaps it would not be too much to say that the most crucial problems of the individual and of society turn upon the way the psyche functions in regard to spirit and matter.
—C.G. Jung

Great Mother Nature has proved most potent...own to the present day. It is "she" who does nothing by leaps, abhors a vacuum, is *die gute Mutter,* is red in tooth and claw, "never did betray the heart that loved her," eliminates the unfit, surges to ever higher and higher forms of life, decrees, purposes, warns, punishes and consoles...Of all the pantheon Great Mother Nature has... been the hardest to kill.
—C.S. Lewis

I

We are trying to present the puer within a structure that recognizes it primarily as a spiritual phenomenon. We would differentiate puer, hero, and son, and, contrary to the classical analytical view, we would suggest that the son who succumbs and the hero who overcomes both take their definition through the relationship with the magna mater, whereas the puer takes its definition from the senex-puer polarity. The young dominant of rising consciousness that rules the style of the ego personality can be determined by the puer (and senex) or by the son and hero

Originally published in *Fathers and Mothers: Five Papers on the Archetypal Background of Family Psychology* (New York: Spring Publications, 1973) and revised in 2005 for inclusion in *UE3: Senex & Puer.*

(and goddess). Nonetheless, analytical psychology has for the most part taken for granted that puer and great mother belong together: the puer-man has, or is, a mother-complex. The puer succumbs to the mother; the hero fights and overcomes her.[1]

Henderson makes one distinction worth noting—and refuting. He associates only the negative *puer aeternus* with the mother-complex and rightly points to the faulty anima relationship, a main psycholog-

---

1. Jung's main remarks directly on the *puer aeternus* in relation with the mother-complex are in *CW*5: §393: "The lovely apparition of the *puer aeternus* is, alas, a form of illusion. In reality he is a parasite on the mother, a creature of her imagination, who only lives when rooted in the maternal body." Cf. §§392, 394, 526 (but also passim in that volume on the mother's son and the hero) and *CW*13, §36 ("provisional life"). In *CW*9.1, "Psychological Aspects of the Mother Archetype," "The Psychology of the Child Archetype," and "On the Psychology of the Trickster Figure" are important for puer psychology in relation with and distinction from the mother. In *CW*13, "The Spirit Mercurius" is useful for some puer phenomenology independent of the mother-complex. For classical cases of the mother-complex in the son, see, for instance, *CW*7, §167ff. and also Jolande Jacobi, "Symbols in an Individual Analysis," in *Man and His Symbols*, edited by C.G. Jung (London: Aldus, 1964), 272ff. This last case might look quite different were it to have been viewed through the eyes of the puer-senex constellation.

Following Jung's early (pre-alchemical) view of the puer would be Marie-Louise von Franz: "With the concept of the eternal youth, *puer aeternus*, we in psychology describe a definite form of neurosis in men, which is distinguished by a fixation [*Steckenbleiben*] in the age of adolescence as a result of an all too strong mother-bind. The main characteristics are therefore those corresponding with Jung's elaborations in his essay on the mother archetype" ("Über religiöse Hintergründe des Puer-Aeternus Problems"), in *The Archetype*, edited by Adolf Guggenbühl-Craig (Basel: Karger, 1964), 141 (trans. mine); and Joseph L. Henderson, *Thresholds of Initiation* (Middletown, Conn.: Wesleyan University Press, 1967), 24: "We may conjecture that when things go wrong with the archetype of the *puer aeternus*, it is because the mother is too demanding or too rejecting, thus frustrating the youth in his normal orientation to the feminine principle as anima-function, or because the youth for some other reason falls into a passive-dependent attitude upon the mother or her substitute." In the same vein: Erich Neumann and M. Esther Harding, whose works are cited below in the relevant places, and also G.F. Heyer, "Die große Mutter im Seelenleben des heutigen Menschen," *Eranos Yearbook* 6 (1938): 454, 474. For intimations of a new view of the puer, this time in connection with Artemis (rather than the mother): René Malamud, "The Amazon Problem," in *Facing the Gods*, edited by James Hillman (Thompson, Conn.: Spring Publications, 2022 [1980]); Thomas Moore, "Artemis and Puer," in *Puer Papers*, edited by James Hillman (Thompson, Conn.: Spring Publications, 2025 [1979]).

ical lacuna of the puer-man. But, because he derives this anima peculiarity from the mother-complex, his view, too, begins and ends with early Jung: puer consciousness is a function of a mother-bound psychology. Henderson's distinction between a "positive" and a "negative" *puer aeternus* is anyway suspect, since it divides in the morality of mind what is not divided in the reality of psyche. Positive and negative signs affixed to psychic events offer the illusion that there are positive and negative aspects of an archetype *per se* and that the plus or minus signs we attribute are valid descriptions. But the signs are relative, placed there by the fantasy of the ego, its decisions in terms of its values and realities. Jung never let us forget that the psyche's opposites contain each other, so that every virtue can be a vice, or vice a virtue. To declare a complex negative is to freeze it in hell. What can it do; where can it go? Not only does the idea of positive and negative puer need rethinking, but also the crucial question of the puer in relation with the mother needs fresh examination.

II

In classical mythology this special entanglement of spirit and maternal world is depicted by the Great Goddess and her young male consort— her son, her lover, her priest. Attis, Adonis, Hippolytus, Phaethon, Tammuz, Endymion, Oedipus are examples of this erotic bind.[2] Each figure

---

2. Not all young male figures show the same pattern. For instance: Hercules is threatened by Hera and even complains of being driven mad by her, while Icarus is altogether with the father; Ganymede and Hyacinthus are loved by male figures, Zeus and Apollo. The interest of the mothers in Achilles, Theseus, and Perseus is more protective than erotic, so, too, in the Nordic, Baldur, and in Moses, Jacob, and Jesus. In these latter examples, where protection and pushing the son forward are the mother's concern, the entanglement through incestuous libido is not the paramount theme. Each mythologem tells another story. The differences are more important for an individual destiny than are the generalizations about the "mother-complex."

There are as well differences among the heroes. Various types have been sorted out: messianic hero, culture hero, suffering martyr, trickster, etc. Just as the word "hero" of mythology has become the word "ego" of psychology, so there is a variety of heroic styles as there is a variety of ego styles. What is characteristic of both hero and ego is the central importance of action. Action may be expressed

in each tale shows its own variation; the Oedipus complex is but one pattern of son and mother that produces those fateful entanglements of spirit with matter that in the twentieth century we have learned to call neurotic. The very desperation of neurosis shows how strong are their mutual needs and that the attempts to untie this primary knot are truly in the ancient sense agonizing and tragic. The primary knot of spirit and matter is personified in the clinging embrace of mother and son.

Alchemy—the fullest and most precise background yet worked out for the processes of analytical work—presents a seemingly similar motif: the extraction of spirit from matter and then their reunion. But the tradition of alchemy pairs the puer figures mainly with the senex (as the young and old Mercurius, as Christ *puer-et-senex*, as King and King's Son), *not* with the mother!

There are many alchemists and many alchemies. There are dragons, devourings, and dissolutions. The material at the beginning is often female and the child at the end often male. Nevertheless, the Great Goddess (as *materia prima*) is not the primary constellating factor of the *puer aeternus* of renewal. The divine child who is called *renovatus in novum infantum, puellus regius, filius philosophorum* is a new spirit born of an old spirit. The process is rather male to male to hermaphrodite and only takes place within the female as material and vessel. There seems a subtle and yet crucial difference between the alchemical conception of the movement of the spirit (puer) and this same movement in hero myths and heroic fairytales. There the hero is unthinkable without his opposition to a Great Goddess or Dragon Witch in one form or another.

Spirit seems differently imagined in alchemy, implying a different theory of neurosis and of psychic movement. In the hero myths, the psyche moves mainly by means of the will into an enlargement of rational order. In alchemy, it seems to be an enlargement of imagination, a

---

by deeds, by importance of honor and reputation, by a remarkable journey or, in reverse, by desolate, impotent suffering. For action the specific psychological attitude of literalizing is necessary. Both hero and ego—no matter the variety of styles and differences between, say, the Venus-hero and the Mars-hero and the Apollo-hero—require a literalization of the challenge. The maiden must be won, the dragon fought, the culture produced, the death accomplished. Literalism, in my view, is a more fundamental trait of hero psychology than the compulsion to act.

freeing of fantasy from various imprisoning literalizations. When Jung shifted the main analogy for the individuation process from the hero myth in *Symbols of Transformation* (in German, 1911) to *Psychology and Alchemy* (in German, Eranos lectures 1936 and 1937), one result was also a shift from the rational and voluntary faculties of the soul to its third faculty, the imagination or *memoria*.[3]

There may be many historical and philosophical reasons for alchemy's presentation of the puer without the great mother as main counterpart, not the least of them being the Christian doctrine of a God who is both Father and Son. Besides these influences upon alchemy's formulations of the puer, more significant are the spontaneous fantasies of the psyche as expressed in alchemical formulations about redemption. In alchemy, too, the embrace of spirit and matter is a suffering and an evil, or what we now call neurotic. However, the way out of this embrace is different. It is not only in terms of a heroic mother-son battle for which St. George and the Dragon has become the major Western paradigm. In alchemy, the dragon is also the creative Mercurius and a figuration (or prefiguration) of the puer. The alchemical hero is devoured by the dragon, or, we would say, imagination takes over. Then comes the activity of discrimination from within the belly where *nous* separates and makes distinctions within the literalizations of *physis*, the physically concrete fantasies. This process of discrimination is imaged in alchemy as cutting through the belly of the beast from within.

Moreover, the myth of the hero is but one motif of alchemy's hundreds, but one way of proceeding, one operation useful at a specific moment or within one constellation; whereas the myth of the hero in modern psychology has become *the* dominant interpretative background for puer psychology.

In yet another way there is a difference between our usual heroic-ego way of thinking about spirit and matter (puer and mother) and the images of alchemy. There, spirit is not mainly presented within a Darwinian fantasy. The pattern is not usually one of generation, spirit born out of maternal matter. The alchemical techné aims at another kind of

---

3. Cf. my discussion of this theme in both *The Myth of Analysis* (Evanston: Northwestern University Press, 1972), 169–90, and in *Re-Visioning Psychology* (New York: Harper & Row, 1975).

relationship between *materia* and *spiritus* where polarities become complementaries, different but equal and joined, as king and queen—and where the close union is *an incest that is a virtue.* Oedipus is altogether irrelevant here, because the entire process is not heroic, not literalized, and not viewed from ego-consciousness. The alchemical representation of development seems never to depart from the unity of the archetype; development of puer consciousness is not *away* from or *against* matter (mother) but always a mercurial business involved with her; *puer-et-senex* needs matter for its foil, for its stuff, for its physicality that gives to its imagination literal materials upon which to fantasy.

We might consider alchemy, then, to be a discipline that is not conceived within the mother complex because its view of spirit is not conceived as a derivative of matter. Its psychology differs from the psychology of science, and so alchemy and science offer different backgrounds to psychology. Because the science fantasy implies mastering matter, science works within the archetype of the great mother. And when we look at the psyche scientifically, our consciousness tends to become appropriated by the archetypal great mother. The alchemist-fantasy is less bound by the "laws" of matter and by quantitative considerations. Qualitative change and precision of it are more important. The alchemical way through the material of the mother is the discipline of fantasy, and alchemical psychology is dominated by the puer-senex pair, its tensions and problems, and its relation with anima.

III

In our lives the mother/son complex is the personalized formulation (within that family language so fondly constellated by the very same mother/son archetype) of the matter-spirit relation. "Mother complex" is another way of stating that spirit cannot present itself, has no effect or reality, except in regard to matter. It only knows itself in contradistinction to matter. If the spirit is heroic, the contradistinction is presented as opposition; if it is materialistic and worldly, it is in that complex's service. Either way its first fascination is with the transformation of matter, earth shakers, world movers, city planners; spiritual acts are materialized in some aspect of concrete reality. The "mother complex" is such a widespread neurosis, spirit is so immersed in the body of matter, delighting there or squirming to shake free, that we can hardly discover other interpretations of spirit—such as the alchemical—except within a polarity to matter. Whenever we think of spirit in these terms, we are "in the mother complex."

Is there not another spirit—or other spirits—of nature, or of the seas, the woods and mountains, of fiery volcanoes or of the underworld that comes from the lower gods (Poseidon, Dionysus, Hades, Hephaestus, Pan), which are male—or hermaphroditic? And is there not a Hermes and a Zeus Chthonios? Must everything below, of nature and of darkness, be mother? The spirit can discover itself by means of another spirit, male with male as parallels, or friends and enemies; so, too, the spirit can have as opposite and partner the soul or the body, neither of which must be the Great Goddess. We may question even whether the spirit can know itself, become conscious, within the mother-son polarity. The blindness of Oedipus would indicate the contrary. If psychology is to free itself for other fantasies for comprehending the psyche's immense range of events, it must first free the puer from the mother, else the spirit of psychology can do nothing better than repeat and confirm what mother has told it to do.

Neurosis cannot be separated from *Weltanschauung*, which always is an expression of one or another variety of the spirit-matter issue and is thus loaded with the archetypal problematics of the great mother/puer relation. Hence the therapists of neurosis, as Jung pointed out, are and must be also doctors of philosophy.[4] The puer/great mother relation is also a philosophical problem that can be expressed in philosophical language. The puer cannot be a functioning psychological organ without having its ideational effects. If therapists of neurosis are doctors of philosophy, they should be able to see not only the neurotic in all philosophy but also the philosophical in all neurosis. Metaphysical ideas are hardly independent of their complex roots; so ideas can be foci of sickness, part of an archetypal syndrome. For example, is not the materialism of some natural science a philosophy of matriarchy in which the scientist willy-nilly becomes a priestly or a heroic son? Does not Vedanta and its transcendence of matter reflect a spirit so entangled in the great world mother that it must resort to disciplined exercises to find liberation? In our metaphysics we state our fantasies about the physical and transcendence of it. A metaphysical statement can be

---

4. *CW* 16, §181.

taken as a psychological fantasy about the matter-spirit relation. These statements are fantasies whose author is the "archetypal neurosis" of puer and mother, reflected in philosophy by the terms spirit and matter. The archetypal neurosis is collective, affecting everyone with a metaphysical affliction. Working out this affliction is individual, which makes therapy a metaphysical engagement in which ideas and not only feelings and complexes undergo process and change. The appearance of puer figures, particularly in the dreams of women, brings new impetus and new struggles also in the realm of ideas, indicating transformations of *Weltanschauung* in regard to all that is included by the term *physis*.

IV

Now we must inquire more precisely into this archetypal contamination of mother and puer. What occurs when the puer as a fundamental structure of the psyche loses its self-identity, its position within the senex-puer whole, and is subtly replaced by the figure of the mother's son?

When the father is absent, we fall more readily into the arms of the mother. And indeed the father is missing; God is dead. We cannot go backward by propping up senex religion. The missing father is not your or my personal father. He is the absent father of our culture, the viable senex who provides not daily bread but spirit through meaning and order.[5] The missing father is the dead God who offered a focus for spiritual things.

Unable to go backward to revive the dead father of tradition, we go downward into the mothers of the collective unconscious, seeking an all-embracing comprehension. We ask for help in getting through the narrow straits without harm; the son wants invulnerability. Grant us protection, foreknowledge; cherish us. Our prayer is to the night for a dream, to a love for understanding, to a little rite or exercise for a moment of wisdom. Above all we want assurance through a vision beforehand that it will all come out all right. Here is the motif of protec-

---

5. Concerning the father (and the senex) as meaning and order, see Chapter 9 below. See also Augusto Vitale, "Saturn: The Transformation of the Father," in this volume, and Luigi Zoja, *The Father: Historical, Psychological and Cultural Perspectives*, translated by Henry Martin (Philadelphia: Brunner-Routledge, 2001).

tion again and a protection of a specific sort: invulnerability, foresight, guarantee that all shall be well, no matter what.

Just here we catch one glimpse of a difference between puer and son. Existential guarantees are given by mothers. Loyalty to her gives her loyalty in return. She won't let you down if you remain loyal to her. Mother assures safety and gives life, but mother does not give true spirit that comes from uncertainty, risk, failure—aspects of the puer. The son does not need the father, whereas the puer seeks recognition from the father, a recognition of spirit by spirit that leads to eventual fatherhood in the puer itself. As we cannot get to the father through the mother, so we cannot get to the hot sperm seed of logos through its imitations in moon magic.

Psychology is not dissolution into psychic magic; psychology is a *logos* of the psyche; it requires spirit. Psychology advances not only through philosophies of the mother: evolution in growth and development, naturalism, materialism, the social adaptation of a feeling-loaded humanism, comparisons with the animal realm, reductions to emotional simplicities like love, sexuality, and aggression. Psychology requires other patterns for advancing its thought and other archetypal carriers, such as the puer, that might liberate psychology's speculative fantasy and insist upon psychology's spiritual significance.

Without the father we lose also the capacity that the Church recognized as "discrimination of the spirits:" the ability to know a call when we hear one and to discriminate between the voices, an activity so necessary for a precise psychology of the unconscious. But the spirit that has no father has no guide for such niceties. The senex-puer division puts an end to spiritual discrimination; instead we have promiscuity of spirits (astrology, yoga, spiritual philosophies, cybernetics, atomic physics, Jungianism, etc.—all enjoyed currently) and the indiscrimination among them of an all understanding mother. The mother encourages her son: go ahead, embrace it all. For her, all equals everything. The father's instruction, on the contrary, is: all equals nothing—unless the all be precisely discriminated.

The realm of the Great Goddess is characterized by the passive inertia and compulsive dynamus of nature; the protective, nourishing, generative cycle in animal and plant from seed to death; an affinity for beauty, timelessness, and emotionality; a preference for opacity, obscurity, coagulation, and darkness; a mystique of the blood *per se* or in kinship ties.[6] All these areas under the domination of the Great Goddess, with but a slight shift of emphasis toward the spiritual, could as well be reflected by the puer. Thus, the puer impulse is *exaggerated* by the mother complex. A contamination of any two archetypes may reinforce them both, or it may depotentiate one in favor of the other.[7] In the special case of the mother-puer confluence, the mother seems to win out, not only by depotentiating spirit but by exaggerating it. Mother, as giver and nourisher, as natural life itself, supplies the puer with an overdose of energetic supplies, and by reinforcing certain of the puer's basic traits she claims him as her dependent son.

When the mother gets hold of these traits, she draws them in extreme. The puer pensiveness becomes an ineffectual daydream; death becomes no longer a terror but a welcomed and natural comfort; laming, instead of an opening into human vulnerability, is turned exaggeratedly by mother into a castration, a paralysis, a suicide. The vertical flights so authentic to the root of the puer become instead a contemptuous soaring over a corrupt and shoddy world; the family problem takes on a religious mystique: all the family members, personages in a matriarchal epic. Then, too, eternity, instead of being an aspect of events and the way in which puer consciousness perceives through to archetypal significance, is distorted into a disregard for time, even a denial of all temporal things. Or a materialistic opportunism appears instead of the genuine puer sense of opportunity, its way of proceeding by hunch and luck, its ambition carried by play and Mercurius. There is materialism too in a peculiar concretism of metaphysical ideas (they must be put in force, acted out in body and clothes and community), in ethics, in sexuality, money, diet, as the mother's matter, repressed, returns in the literalizations of puer abstractions. The cycle of nature (which in puer consciousness is a field out of which to draw metaphors to make jokes upon, play and experiment with) in son consciousness becomes a pious nature "out there," a shack in the woods, soiled clothes, Hatha Yoga; and beauty, which for the puer reflects Platonic ideals and is a revelation of

---

6. "These are three essential aspects of the mother: her cherishing and nourishing goodness, her orgiastic emotionality, and her Stygian depths," and as Jung goes on to say, not "discriminating knowledge" (*CW*9.1, §158).

7. *CW*5, §199.

the essence of value, narrows instead into the vanities of my own image, my own aesthetic productions and sensitivities.

The close association of mother and son in the psyche is imaged as incest and experienced as ecstasy and guilt. The ecstasy goes in both vertical directions, divine and hellward, but the guilt is not assuaged. The great mother changes the puer's debt to the transcendent—what he owes the gods for his gifts—into a debt of feeling, a guilt toward her symbols in the round of material life. He overpays society in family, job, civic duties, and avoids his destiny. Through her, his relation with material life oscillates between ecstatic springing of its binds or guilty submission to them. In the sexual sphere, psychoanalysts have called this "oscillation," the continual back and forth between lust and guilt, guilt and lust.

The ecstatic aspect in a man carried by the conjoined archetype of mother-son takes him yet further from the father's inhibitions of order and limit. Ecstasy is one of the goddess's ways of seducing the puer from its senex connection. By overcoming limit, puer consciousness feels itself overcoming fate, which sets and is limit.[8] Rather than loving fate or being driven by it, the puer escapes from fate in magical, ecstatic flight. Puer aspirations are fed with new fuel: the potent combustible of sexual and power drives whose source is in the instinctual domain of the Great Goddess.[9] These exaggerations of the puer impulse set him afire. He is the torch, the arrow, and the wing, Aphrodite's son Eros. He seems able to realize in his sexual life and his career every wish of his childhood's omnipotence fantasies. It's all coming true. His being is a magic phallus, glowing and strong, every act inspired, every word pregnant with deep, natural wisdom. The Great Goddess behind the scenes has handed him this ecstatic wand. She governs both the animal desire and the horizontal world of matter over which she offers promise of conquest.

Due to the emotionality of the great mother, the dynamus of the son is unusually labile, unusually dependent upon emotion. Inspiration can no longer be differentiated from enthusiasm, the correct and

---

8. Richard Broxton Onians, *The Origins of European Thought* (Cambridge, Mass.: Cambridge University Press, 1954), 349–95.

9. Cf. Joseph Fontenrose, *Python: A Study of Delphic Myth* (Berkeley: University of California Press, 1959), 582, for references to the Venusberg-Siren theme, relevant to the mother-anima contamination.

necessary ascension from ecstasy. The fire flares up and then all but goes out, damp and smoky, clouding vision and afflicting others with the noxious air of bad moods. The dependence of spirit upon mood described in vertical language (heights and depths, glory and despair) has its archetypal counterpart in the festivals for Attis, Cybele's son, which were called *hilaria* and *tristia*.[10]

When the vertical direction toward transcendence is misdirected through the great mother, the puer is no longer authentic. He takes his role now from the relationship with the feminine. Ecstasy and guilt are two parts of the pattern of sonship. Even more important is heroism. Whether as hero-lover, or hero-hermit denying matter but with an ear to nature's breast, or hero conquerer who slays some slimy dragon of public evil, or as Baldur, so perfect and so unable to stanch the bleeding from his beautiful wounds, puer has lost its freedom. Direct access to the spirit is no longer there; it requires drama, tragedy, heroics. Life becomes a performance acted out through a role in the relationship with the eternal feminine who stands behind every such son: martyr, messiah, devotee, hero, lover. By playing these roles, we are part of the cult of the Great Goddess.[11] Our identities are given by the enactment

---

10. "The Roman ceremonies which were held in Attis's honor during the month of March were divided into two principal parts: the tristia, the commemoration of Attis's passion and death, and the hilaria, the festivities of his followers, who believed that the god comes to life again after a long winter sleep" (M.J. Vermaseren, *The Legend of Attis in Greek and Roman Art* [Leiden: E.J. Brill, 1966], 39). Attis is another of the appearing and disappearing gods whose cyclical return has been interpreted as the vegetative rhythm and the *tristia* and *hilaria* ultimately as fertility rituals. By substituting "libido" for "fertility," we can transpose the entire pattern from the external and natural to the internal and psychological level. Then the *tristia* and *hilaria* refer to the rhythm of the libido, the discontinuities (comings and goings) of the puer impulse, at whose appearance we rejoice and feel Spring, and in whose absence there is the sadness of Winter, which Attis too represented (i.e., his senex side). These seasons and this fertility are not just "out there" in nature but "inside" experienced as the natural cycle of psychic energy.

11. Curious how the mother archetype has encroached upon areas that once belonged to other archetypes. The earth in ancient Egyptian mythology was Geb, a god (not a goddess). The sea, taken so stereotypically in the analytical interpretation of dreams as a "symbol for" (hence, "sign of") the collective unconscious as matrix and thus as the maternal element, was once the province of Father Okeanos, who

of these roles and thus we become her sons, since our life depends on the roles she gives. She thus can affect even the way that the puer seeks the senex: exaggerating the discipleship of the student to his master, the swagger of the battler with the old order, the exclusivity of the messiah whose new truth refuses everything that has gone before. The mother-complex dulls *the precision of the spirit*; issues become quickly either/or, since the Great Goddess does not have much comprehension of the spirit. She only grasps it in relationship to her; that is, the mother-complex must make of spirit something *related*. It must have effects in the realm of matter: life, world, people. This sounds "only human" and full of "common sense," again terms too often expressing the sentimentalism of the mother-complex. Even should a man recognize the mother in his actions and take flight from her relatedness into lofty abstraction and vast, impersonal fantasy, he is still the son filled with the animus of the goddess, her pneuma, her breath and wind. And he serves her best by making such divisions between his light and her darkness, his spirit and her matter, between his world and hers.

This is the animus thinking of sonship, found as much in men as women. It is a thinking of coagulations and oppositions between them, rather than a thinking in distinctions between perspectives. For it is not that the mother is this or that and the puer this or that, as describable objects, things, but rather that mother and puer are ways of perceiving. More or less the same "facts" can be found in puer and in the mother's son, so the real difference between them lies in the way in which we perceive these facts. But the mother does not want to be seen through. She throws up her veils of darkness, her opacity and emotionality, and presents crude, materialized divisions between God and Caesar, this world and the next, time and eternity, sacred and profane, introvert and extravert, and so on, *ad infinitum,* keeping her animus-son eternally occupied, preventing his need for an eternality of another sort.

---

was a source of all things (Homer), and the rivers of life were fathering river gods, e.g., Achelous, Poseidon (Helikon). Cf. Karl Kerényi, "Man and Mask" in *Spiritual Disciplines: Papers from the Eranos Yearbooks,* edited by Joseph Campbell (London: Routledge, 1961), 158.

In Jung's English-language *Collected Works,* the only archetype that consistently receives capital letters is the Great Mother, an honoring not offered to the wise old man, anima, animus, or even self; the "gods" and "goddesses" are also written small.

This eternality of the puer would see through all such opposites in terms of their fundamental likeness as a way of thought. The movement from son to puer, that is, the movement of restoration of the original puer vision, occurs when one sees through the challenge of opposites that the Great Goddess embroils us in so that one can refuse to do battle with her in the field of her entangling dilemmas. By this I do not mean that the puer vision is that of a Nietzschean superman, beyond good and evil. Rather I mean that the puer vision, because of its inherent connection with the senex, can live within this field, as the field of necessity, simply by seeing through to the ambiguity that is the identity of opposites. There is no need either to force choices as does the hero-son or to make a theology of conflict in the fashion of the priest-son. The puer vision is transcendent and beyond in the sense that it is not caught in her literal animus-game; therefore, puer consciousness does not have to be literally transcendent, leave the scene, cut out, blow.

V

There is also the anti-hero or hero-in-reverse, who is another puer substitute, another form of the great mother's son. He lives in her lap and off the lap of the land. Rather than all phallus, he is all castration—weak, gentle, yielding to life and its blows. He chooses to lose and his is the soft answer to wrath, which spirit he is unable to meet without the father. His way follows nature, the path of least resistance, eventually into the primeval swamp, bogged. Like water he flows downward, slips out of sight, and has effects underground, so like water that he evokes the divine child in the water rushes. But this son is not separated from the water by cradle, basket, boat; he is the water. He gives the illusion of being on the right way, wending around obstacles, as the Tao is called "water" and "child." But unlike Icarus he does not plunge into the water vertically, nor does he serve Olympian archetypal principles with wet enthusiasm as does Ganymede the cupbearer. He just goes along with what is going, a stream slipping through the great body of mother nature, ending ultimately in the amniotic estuary streaming into oceanic bliss. Whether hyperactive with theatrics or ecstatics, or passive, the flow of energy results from the mother archetype. The anti-hero attempts to resolve the puer-complex through the degradation of energy. The individual follows along, letting things happen, dropping out from the demands put upon the heroic ego. He makes few demands even on himself, wanting little and needing less and less. As tensions equalize he believes himself in rare balance, becoming cooler and less personal. His images and ideas become more archetypal, reflecting universal levels of the collective unconscious.

Because there appears to be a spiritual advance in visual, poetic, and metaphysical ideas, the term "regression" is refused as a misnomer. Regression means return to more childish or historically earlier behavior patterns, but the passive son seems so obviously to be making spiritual advancement toward ever-widening values and general symbols, progressing through the perennial philosophy into truths of all religions—even if requiring sometimes financial support or hallucinogenic reinforcement. One can hardly be "regressing" while quoting Hesse, Don Juan, Gurdjieff, Tagore, Eckhart, Merton, and Socrates! The philosophy, however, has a defensive note providing a wrap-around shield against heroics, will, and effort. For example, the anti-heroics of Ramakrishna, "The nearer you get to God, the less he gives you to do": These traits and the predictable pattern of the anti-hero—what he will do, read, say next—disclose that in his spiritual progress he is actually following the degradation of energy in its entropic direction, which is, in another language as Freud pointed out, Nirvana—or death. The entropy in a system is characterized by cooling and running down, by increase of statistical probability, equalization of tension, generalization (randomness), degradation from higher to lower descriptions of energy, and increasing disorder. All of this appears in individual behavior as well as in the behavior of any complex when it "gives up."

Although the theme of "giving up" belongs in another chapter, we may note a difference between the puer and the hero or antihero in this respect. The puer gives up because of an inadequate survival sense. Separated from the senex, it does not know how to defend itself or keep itself in order. The hero/anti-hero gives up owing to the mother. It would free psychic energy by getting rid of complexes altogether. But, as Jung points out, complexes are the mother of psychic energy, so to conquer them, overcome them, or cure oneself of them, is another way of trying to rid oneself of the mother.

Puer and hero also differ in their self-destructiveness. The puer is self-destructive because it lacks psyche—containment, reflection, involvement. And it lacks, when separated from the senex, the ability to father itself, to put a roof over its head and a wall around its property. The self-destructiveness of the puer in any complex arises because the complex does not understand itself: it sees, it knows, it makes—but it does not see or know or make itself. There is an absence of psychic reflection of the spirit and an absence of spiritual realization within the psyche.

The hero is self-destructive because it would have done with the complex, and this may occur in various ways. It may appear as eros idealism, the inspiration of transforming the complexes into wholeness. It may appear as anti-heroic cooling of the complexes, depotentiating everything of tension (or its reverse, burning everything up in enthusiasm). It may appear as the cure of loving acceptance—which is also a death-wish, revealing how close eros and thanatos are to each other. For to be healed and made whole by love or to give up the tension by death are close indeed. Both refuse the complex as the fundamental necessity of psychic life, the only cure for which is death. Death alone puts an end to the complexes that are "normal phenomena of life"[12] and like the mother are the fundament of each individual's existence. We are complexed beings, and human nature is a composition of complexities. Without complexes there is no living reality, only a transcendent Nirvana of the Buddha whose last supposed words point to the complexity of the psyche as life's primary given: "Decay is inherent in all composite things—work your salvation with diligence."

Getting rid of and giving up this complexity through any formula for overcoming opposites, or dropping out, or curing misses psychic reality. Psychological therapy is less an overcoming and a getting rid than it is a decay, a decomposing of the way in which we are composed. This the alchemists called the *putrefactio,* the slow time process of transformation through affliction, wastage, and moral horror. Both heroic getting-rid and passive giving-up attempt to speed decay and have done with it; they would avoid the work of psychic reality by escape into spiritual salvation. *But the cure is the decay.*

When the puer lives authentically to its structure, there is this smell of decadence, a fond attachment to one's mess, which is part of its resistance to analysis. In this sense the puer—seemingly so quick and flame-

---

12. *CW*8: 211, 213.

like—is slow to change, shows no development, seems forever stuck in the same old dirty habits. His putrefaction is in his intractable symptoms of colon and digestion, of eczema and acne, of piles, in his long, slow colds and sinuses, his chronic genital complaints, his money peculiarities, or in his low-life fascinations. These things analysis has wrongly attributed to the shadow repression owing to the mother-complex: he is bound to the mother in a compensatory materialistic way and cannot fight free. But against the background of decay, the slowness and the dirt in the puer can be seen as a way of following the path of putrefaction toward finding the outcast senex. As such it is a digestive, fermentative process that should not be heroically hurried. Nor should rot be forcefully "rubbed in" as a treatment to integrate the shadow. The puer is not a dog; puer consciousness needs not house-breaking and heeling but a new attunement of his sensitivity to the odors of his own decay. His individuation is in the pathologizing process itself and not in his heroic efforts to overcome.

We can anyway not rid ourselves of complexes until they have given us up. Their decaying time is longer than the life of the individual personality, since they continue in a kind of autonomous existence long after we have left the scene; they are part of the psychic inheritance of our children and their children, both natural and spiritual. The complexes are our dosage of sin, our karma, which if given up is really only passed on elsewhere. In the analysis of those men called "puer," one needs a nose for decay, for waste, for moldering ruin. By nursing the mess along we keep the puer alive and in touch with the *prima materia*; by whitewashing with bland acceptance (giving-up) or hurrying the process to get going (getting-rid), we put the authentic spirit into the old bottle marked "Mother."

VI

In our consideration of puer and mother we should look, if only briefly, at Dionysus.[13] He has, of course, been perceived as a typical mother's

---

13. The best short treatment of Dionysus in English is that of Walter F. Otto, *Dionysus: Myth and Cult*, translated by Robert B. Palmer (Bloomington: Indiana University Press, 1981). The most complete is Karl Kerényi, *Dionysos: Archetypal Image of Indestructible Life*, translated by Ralph Manheim (Princeton, N.J.: Princeton University Press, 1976). I have given further literature on Dionysus in my *The Myth of Analy-*

son. The nurses, the milk, the emotionality, the dance, his unheroic behavior and weaponlessness, his softness and effeminacy, the women's favorite—all this has meant to our simple, so-called psychological minds nothing but one more striking archetypal example of the mother-complex.[14]

But Dionysus may also be seen within the puer-senex structure. His name means Zeus-Son; his mythologems are in many aspects almost interchangeable with those of the Cretan Zeus, and in one of his birth performances he is delivered from the thigh of his father, male born of male. It is questionable whether we may call Dionysus puer in our modern psychological sense, even though *puer* was one of his Latin epithets. But since Dionysus was one of the young gods and since his cult pre-

---

sis, 258–81 and have reviewed how Jung regards this figure in my "Dionysos in Jung's Writings."

14. Neumann, whose main line of thinking (feeling?) is within the mother archetype, of course places Dionysus in her train. He speaks of Leonardo's painting of Bacchus as a portrayal of the *puer aeternus*: "The relaxed and indolent way in which the hermaphroditic god sits resting in the countryside is wholly in keeping with the ancient conception of Dionysus...Leonardo, unconsciously no doubt, portrayed a central figure of the matriarchal mystery world, closely related to the vulture goddess. For Dionysus is the mystery god of feminine existence." He continues this for several paragraphs; his point is that Dionysus is another "divine luminous son of the Great Mother" (Erich Neumann, "Leonardo and the Mother Archetype," in his *Art and the Creative Unconscious,* translated by Ralph Manheim [New York: Pantheon, 1959], 70). I would not disabuse the reader from Neumann's view: any archetype may be viewed from within any perspective so that Dionysian events may well be seen as matriarchal. I would only disabuse the reader from Neumann's argument, as if it were based on evidence. The vulture has nothing to do either with Dionysus or with the puer; Egypt is only one of many "alien" and "border" areas from which Dionysus and his cult were said to spring; Dionysus did not come "late to Greece" (Neumann) but appears even in the early Cretan culture. Mythical statements about archetypes are anyway to be read mythically, psychologically, and not historically, literally.

There is a significant difference between Jung and Neumann in regard to the puer nature of Dionysus. Although Jung does once place Dionysus (Iacchus/Zagreus) as a *puer aeternus* within the Eleusinian mystery cult, and thus within the mother archetype (*CW*5, §526–27), he noted already in 1911 (ibid., §184): "The double figure of the adult and infant Dionysus..." speaking of him in the context of the "giant and dwarf," "big and little," "father and son." Thus Jung saw what Neumann did not: Dionysus is himself a *senex-et-puer* and can as well be regarded from this perspective as from within that of the mother.

sented him, especially in later antiquity, in child form,[15] he shows some traits relevant for our thoughts here, even if the quality of his masculinity differs from what our historical consciousness under its Greco-Roman and Judeo-Christian heroic dominants has decided is masculine. So we have written off "the Dionysian" to the mother; therewith we have missed the spiritual significance implied by Dionysus *puer*, and we have misappreciated the wine, the theatrical and its tragedy, the style of madness and phallicism, and other aspects of his nature and cult that bear on puer consciousness. Puer may find in Dionysus a background to traits and experiences that are not to be taken literally and acted out in dancing troops with tambourines but which offer another and softer means for the puer-senex, father-son, reunion. Dionysus presents the spiritual renewal in nature or the natural renewal of the spirit, encompassing in himself the cyclical and generative traits of mother nature with the culture, inspiration, and irrational excitement of puer consciousness.

Dionysus, they say, has several mothers. Demeter, Io, Dione, Persephone, Lethe, and Semele have been variously named. And the relationship between his mothers is *discontinuous*. Semele is killed by Zeus while still pregnant; Zeus is his second mother; he is mothered by nymphs in a cave, by Persephone, by his grandmother Rhea, who puts back together his dismembered pieces.

This discontinuity in the mother is not exclusive to Dionysus. Other gods and heroes are "motherless," i.e., abandoned, suckled by animals, raised by foster mothers or nurses, the natural mother having disappeared or died. Psychoanalysis has made much of this theme of "the two mothers." It has become the good and bad breast; and Jung, too, devoted a large piece of his *Symbols of Transformation* to "The Dual Mother," by which is meant two sides of the same figure, a positive life-cherishing and a negative life-endangering aspect.

But I would look at the two (or more) mothers from another angle, not as different kinds or faces of one figure, but as an interruption in the relation between mother and child. I suggest that the rupture in natural continuity (Semele's not carrying the child to term) offers another way

---

15. Cf. Martin P. Nilsson, "The Dionysiac Mysteries of the Hellenistic and Roman Age," *Skrifter utgivna av Svenska institutet i Athen* 8, no. 5 (1957): 111.

of regarding the relation between *mater* and *puer.* Owing to the inter-vention of Zeus's thunderbolt—or whatever other spiritual inroad into the natural continuity between mother and son, whether from Pharaoh in the Moses tale or from the oracle in the case of Oedipus—the son does not have to force a break with the mother. It has happened. It is given with his condition. He is no longer only her child. The only-natu-ral has been broken because the spiritual has intervened, and so a sepa-ration of puer consciousness from mother occurs without the necessity of cutting or killing. Evidently, another archetype is activated to which the son also belongs, and this other archetype is as signal to his fate as is the mother from whom he is separated.

To make this point more clear let us turn to Leonardo da Vinci. The critical event in his early memory (as Freud and Neumann[16] have writ-ten) was indeed the bird that descended to him in the cradle. Leon-ardo lived with his grandmother and with two successive stepmothers; his natural mother married again and seems to have disappeared from Leonardo's life. Leonardo has a fantasy, which he recounts as if it were an actual memory from infancy, that a *nibio,* opened his mouth with its tail and struck him many times upon his lips. This bird was not a vulture, as Freud and then Neumann have declared. Neumann, despite notic-ing that a *nibio* is *not* a vulture and so correcting Freud's error, none-theless sustains it by retaining the mistranslation as symbolically cor-rect in order to analyze, along with Freud, Leonardo in terms of the mother-complex.[17]

---

16. Sigmund Freud, "Leonardo da Vinci and a Memory of His Childhood," in *SE* 11; Erich Neumann, "Leonardo and the Mother Archetype" in *Art and the Creative Uncon-scious,* translated by Ralph Manheim (New York: Pantheon, 1959).

17. Neumann, "Leonardo," 14: "Against the background of archetypal relations, the bird of Leonardo's childhood fantasy, considered in its creative uroboric unity of breast-mother and phallus-father, is symbolically a 'vulture' even if Leonardo called it a 'nibio'...For this reason we are perfectly justified in retaining the term 'vulture,' which Freud chose 'by mistake,' for it was through this very 'blunder' that his keen intuition penetrated to the core of the matter..."; i.e., "the symbolic equation vulture = mother," ibid., 7).

This vulture was "seen" by Oskar Pfister in Leonardo's painting of St. Anne with Virgin and Christ Child as a negative form in the blue cloth that drapes and links the figures. Jung, too, "saw" a vulture in that painting. In a letter to Freud of 17 June 1909, Jung writes that he has seen a vulture (*Geier* in German) in a different place from the one seen by Pfister. Jung's vulture has its "beak precisely in the pubic region."

No. The bird, which came to Leonardo in his vision, was a kite, a relative of the hawk and like it a variety of the genus *falconidae*. (Hawk is the wider term, kite one of its varieties.) We have here to do with a symbol that can best be amplified from Egypt where Freud turned for his symbolic equation vulture = mother. But it is now the equation: hawk, kite, falcon = Horus = puer. The solar hawk descended upon the Kings at their coronation and was a spirit-soul (*ka*), and the hawk in a series of other contexts is a puer emblem *par excellence*.

Because of the specific puer significance of this bird, the dual mother theme in Leonardo, on which Freud and Neumann base their interpretative case of his genius, may rather, and more correctly, be understood in terms of a discontinuity in the mother relation owing to the early intervention of the puer archetype in its apparition as a kite and which Leonardo kept as a valued memory. (I have not examined the biographical material enough to tell whether the intervention of the *nibio* image occurred precisely at a time between two of his many mothers. But I do not think the literal aspect of discontinuity is as important as are the two factors: the intervention of the puer and the discontinuity in mothers.)

Leonardo's interest in flying, his love of birds, as well as his supposed vegetarianism and homosexuality, may thus have a "hawk" in the background rather than a "vulture" and may be grasped as part of puer phenomenology rather than as a mother complex. The various usages of the word "kite" in English emphasize the puer implications. A kite is a flying, triangular, light framed toy, a favorite of small boys, and a kite is "one who preys upon others." The term refers also to the highest sails of a ship that are set only in a light wind.

Strachey, who edited Freud's works for the *Standard Edition*, said the hidden vulture idea must be abandoned in the light of the kite-hawk-falcon (*nibio*), which was Leonardo's actual bird. But Neumann responds to this by saying that, in Pfister, Freud, and in Leonardo too, "the symbolic image of the Great Mother proved stronger than the actual image of the 'kite'" (*SE*11: 64–66). The power of the archetypal image of the Great Mother certainly dominated the psychoanalytic interpretation in all these commentators, but this does not establish that it also dominated Leonardo in the same way.

For a succinct devastation of Freud's Leonardo thesis, based on the vulture-kite confusion, see David E. Stannard, *Shrinking History: On Freud & the Failure of Psychohistory* (New York: Oxford University Press, 1980), 5–21.

Moreover, the "case" of Leonardo seems paradigmatic for both archetypal psychology in general and the psychology of genius in particular. By ignoring the true significance of an image (in this case the hawk-falcon-kite), one can attribute a crucial event of any life wrongly to an inappropriate archetypal constellation. Then genius is not viewed authentically in terms of the spirit and its early call but is rather attributed to peculiarities in the fate of the mother. Because the vulture-or-kite quarrel stands for the conflict in perspectives between mother and puer, we can see how important an investment early psychoanalysis had in the mother archetype and how there was a consequent misperception and repression of the puer that is only now beginning to be revalued...A lesson we may draw from the Dionysus and the Leonardo examples is that what we see is determined by how we look, which is in turn determined by where we stand.

VII

When we stand within the consciousness influenced mainly by the great mother, all puer phenomena seem derivative of the mother complex, and even our consciousness itself becomes "her son," a resultant of the primordial matrix of the unconscious. Yet, there is no such thing as "the mother-complex." If we are strict and are not just led along by easy language, complexes do not belong to any specific archetype. The complexes—power, money, illness, sex, fear, ambition, jealousy, self-destruction, knowledge, etc.—which form the energetic cores and provide the fantasy stuff of our afflictions and transformations do not belong to any single god.

First, there are no single gods. In polytheism, each god implies and involves others. *Theos* and *deus* (as well as the Celtic and Nordic roots of our God consciousness) arise in a polytheistic context where reference to God always meant a field of many gods. A single God without others is unthinkable. Even our Judeo-Christian second commandment makes this statement, albeit in a negative fashion ("Thou shalt have no other gods before me"). Second, the gods interpenetrate, as the archetypes interfuse. The archetypes do not so much rule realms of being as they, like the gods, rule all at once and together the same realm of being, this our world. But they provide distinctions within this world, different ways of regarding things, different patterns for psychizing instinct, different modes of consciousness. So, third, complexes are not assigned either by definition or by nature to specific archetypal patterns. Any complex may at one time or another be under the aegis of this or that dominant, and any dominant may at any time take over this or that complex. For example, money may seem to belong to Saturn's greed, he who coined money, or to Mercurius the trader, or to the hero's booty, or to Zeus who can appear as a shower of gold; or it may be the gold of Apollo, or belong within the Midas constellation; or money may even point a way into the psychic underworld, for Hades's other name was Pluto (wealth). So, too, for sexuality, which takes on altogether different characteristics when Apollonic, Dionysian, Priapian, or in the service of Hera.[18]

Even the puer's orality—seemingly that one complex so certainly belonging to the mother archetype—may be envisioned otherwise. Psychology has surprisingly little to say about taste, food, hunger, eating. All are swallowed up in "orality." Ever since the "oral stage" was laid out by Freud, everything to do with mouth, stomach, with food and cooking and drinking, with hungers of every sort goes back to Mom and her breasts (or bottle). But puer food behavior can show an asceticism, for instance, of a Pythagorean-Orphic sort. It can show a sensitivity in aesthetic flavors that belong (in the magical-astrological tradition of *Picatrix*) to Venus and not the Moon. Or, the puer hunger for more belongs more properly to Saturn and his greed, the wolf, Moloch, Bhoga, a rapacious eating of the world.

The shift of archetypal background to a complex is a common enough experience when a problematic and habitual knot is suddenly released and a wholly new perspective is disclosed. It is as if the complex has been redeemed by the grace, or the viewpoint, of a different god. We are equally familiar with the reverse: when a virtue suddenly is experienced through another archetype and becomes now "destructive" and a "shadow problem." Sometimes this shift from one archetype to another occurs as a breakdown. What previously supported one's ego-complex—say the nymphic anima, or the flaming, inspiring eros, or

---

18. For a more thorough sketch of the mobility of the complex among different archetypal dominants and their perspectives, see my *The Myth of Analysis*, 40–49, where I present the notion (and complex) of creativity as it can be experienced by seven different archetypal structures.

the conservative self-righteousness of moralistic Saturn—withdraws its domination. Then, a collapse and revolution take place until the complex can recognize its new Lord and find new archetypal sanction.

By giving over any complex to a single archetype, we condemn it to a single view, a diagnosis made too often in analysis. (This is your spiritual animus, your negative father, your neglected child, etc.) This frustrates the movement of the complex among the gods, fixating it by definition and frustrating its Hermetic possibilities for transformation through movement of perspective. When we fix a complex to only one archetype, only one sort of insight can arise. It is crucially important to view moodiness, for example, not only as typically puer but also as typically anima, typically mother, and also as a power trick of the shadow, and even of the senex. As Eros does not belong only to Aphrodite because there are many kinds of loving, and as fighting can be governed by Ares, Athene, Nike, Apollo, Hercules, and Amazons, and as madness can be brought on and taken away by a variety of dominants, so may any complex be a tributary of the great mother and yet at the same time accord with the puer-senex.

By this I do not intend to deny complex, negative maternal phenomena. The "negative mother" appears in the myths of destructive femininity (Hecate, Gorgo, Kali, Lua, and the other Great Goddesses who consume and lay waste). She is also evident in the barrenness of collective kindness, structures without milk, customs without tradition in a civilization that offers no support, nothing natural. The "negative mother" is visible in the voices of the women with their children, the faces of ugly mouths and flat eyes, the resentment and hatred. It is a wonder anyone survives at all through the early years when mother-love comes with its double, mother-hate. Of course, we live in an age of Moms, for the culture is secular and the ordinary mortal must carry archetypal loads without help from the gods. The mothers must support our survival without support themselves, having to become like goddesses, everything too much, and they sacrifice us to their frustration as we in turn, becoming mothers and fathers, sacrifice our children to the same civilization.

The way to "solve the mother-complex" would be not to cut from Mom but to cut the antagonism that makes me heroic and her negative. To "solve the mother-complex" of the puer means to remove the puer phenomena from the mother, no longer viewing puer problems as mother-caused and mother-bound. (For in our civilization what cannot be blamed on the mother?) Rather than separate man and mother, we need to separate the archetypal necessity of their association and to consider puer phenomena in their own right. Then one can turn to each puer aspect and ask it where it belongs, in accordance with the procedure in ancient Greece when consulting an oracle. "To what god or hero must I pray or sacrifice to achieve such and such a purpose"[19]: To what archetypal pattern do I relate my problem? Within which fantasy can I insight my complex? Once the problem has been placed upon a relevant altar, one can connect with it according to its own needs and connect to the god through it.

By taking for granted that puer phenomena belong to the great mother, *analytical psychology has given the puer a mother-complex.* Puer phenomena have received an inauthentic cast for which the epithet "neurotic" seems justified. By laying the complex on the altar of the great mother, rather than maintaining its connection with the *senex-et-puer* unity, we consume our own spiritual ground, giving over to the goddess our eros, ideals, and inspirations, believing they are ultimately rooted in the maternal, either as my personal mother, or matter, or as a causally conditioned contextual field called society, economics, the family, etc. By making spirit her son, we make spirit itself neurotic. By taking the frailties and youthful follies necessary to all spiritual beginnings merely as infantilisms of the mother-complex, we nip in the bud the possibility of renewal in ourselves and our culture. This view of things serves only to perpetuate the neurosis, preventing the reunion of senex and puer. Puer then seems opposite and enemy of senex, and the age seems rightly characterized by what Freud suggested, a universal Oedipus complex, son against father because of the mother.

In individuals, these distortions of the puer show themselves in the personal mother-complex. In society, there are distortions of spiritual goals and meanings, because an ambitiously heroic ego development has been the recipe for resolution of the puer syndrome. To assume that the puer is primarily the same as the son of the great mother is to confirm the pathological distortions as an authentic state of being. The distortion of puer into son is perpetuated by the mother archetype, which

---

19. H.W. Parke, *Greek Oracles* (London: Hutchinson, 1967), 87.

prefers the hero myth as the model for ego-development since that model depicts the ego to be primarily and necessarily embroiled with her. Our main Western psychological theories rest on a model that more or less declares the dynamics of the psyche to be derivatives of the family and society, which are the preserve of the mother. Psychology itself is her victim, not only in its therapeutics of ego development, but more fundamentally: the spirit of psychology is lamed by materialism, literalism, and a genetic viewpoint toward its own subject matter, the psyche. The spiritual nature and purposes of psychology never emerge because the puer never emerges from the mother. Or it emerges still bound with a navel cord, psychology as a heroic mission of the priest-son whose urge is either to spread self through the world or to become self in disdain of the world.

Psychology, as Jung insisted, always reflects our psychic condition.[20] A psychology that sees mother everywhere is a statement about the psyche of the psychologist and not only a statement based on empirical evidence. To advance the psyche through its collective mother-complex, psychology itself must advance in its self-reflection so that its subject, the soul, is no longer dominated by naturalism and materialism, and the goals for that soul are no longer formulated via the mother archetype as "growth," "social adaptation," "human relatedness," "natural wholeness," etc.

Our ideas about the psyche affect the psyche. Ideas can be poisonous as well as therapeutic. Psychological ideas are particularly important since they tell the psyche about itself, giving a mirror in which to view its own events. Psychological concepts can work as liberating transformers, offering a new view of what had hitherto been condemned or misperceived. As Jung wrote: "Psychology inevitably merges with the psychic process itself"[21]—and, of course, as the psychic process moves it will continue to produce new aspects of psychology. In no other field is the state of the doer more involved with what is done than in psychology. Operator and material are indistinguishable; psychology is alchemy in a new dress. The more complicated and differentiated psychic life becomes, the more anachronistic to go on with sim-

20. *CW* 8, §223.
21. Ibid., §429.

plest accounts in terms of biochemistry, brain physiology, sociology, psychodynamics, family genetics. Moreover, inadequate psychological accounts interfere with psychic differentiation, having a noxious effect on the soul. For this reason, among many others, psychology turns to mythology. Mythic accounts are the most open, most exploratory, most suggestively subtle yet precise, allowing the soul the widest imagination for its complexes.

Yet, mythology for all its precision in detail leaves ambiguities about fundamentals, since the figures themselves, like the archetypes, are *dei ambigui.*[22] We find the figures of hero, puer, and son not distinguished as clearly as our monocular minds would want. Myth offers possibilities for perceiving but not facts for building a case to prove that the puer is this and the son or hero is that. Proof is not the aim of myth; it does not set out to display an argument, to explain, or to demonstrate a single line of thought on any theme. Besides, the great mother is everywhere, because pervasiveness is at the essence of that dominant. So it is not independence from mother that separates puer out from son-hero but independence in our *conception* of the puer.

Perhaps the question—puer or son, authentic spirit or mother-derivative—can never be answered in the form of such sharp alternatives that, too, betray a kind of consciousness that asks questions in terms of swords and sunlight and would codify the psyche into the straight thinking of priestly dogma.

Hero, puer, and son are all the same in one basic respect: *youth.* Youth carries the significance of becoming, of self-correcting growth, of being beyond itself (ideals) since its reals are in *status nascendi.* So it is decisive how we envision this youth, whether embodied in a young person, as a dream figure, or as any young potential of the soul, since this youth is the emergence of spirit within the psyche. Just as there are young gods and heroes, and young men of genius, who cannot all be understood in terms of the Great Goddess, so there are young men and young figures in our dreams who cannot all be interpreted through the mother-complex. Apollo, Hermes, and Dionysus have many typically puer characteristics that cannot be put down to mother, implying an

---

22. Edgar Wind, *Pagan Mysteries in the Renaissance* (Harmondsworth: Penguin, 1967), 196.

authentic puer consciousness based on their authenticity as full and distinct gods. Conversely, there are young men who have true mother-complexes in the sense of modern psychology, yet who do not show authentic puer characteristics. There is no fire, no spirit, no goal; the destructive and renegade tendencies are not present; fantasy is weak, and there is no exaggerated woundedness—distinguishing traits of the puer. So, the ideal therapist of the archetypal persuasion would watch carefully the actual phenomenology. And myth would help him perceive distinctions.

The cosmos in which we place youth and through which we insight youth will influence its pattern of becoming. From the mother's perspective, male youth belongs with the female as a consort, part of her fertility and natural growth, her heroical culture drive, her realm of death. From the senex perspective, male youth is renewal both as hope and as threat, the same and the different in one figure, and a dynamus that calls for order, an innocence asking for knowledge, and a possibility to be realized through time and labor.

Although these two views of youth describe kinds of consciousness, we do not need to make a hierarchy of these kinds, demonstrating that matriarchy is prior to patriarchy or that son, hero, puer reflect levels of development. It is not a matter of which is right in terms of which comes first. We are not concerned with the "origins and history of consciousness" or the origins of son, hero, puer, or of gods. The search for origins has to lead back to the mother anyway who must always come "first," since genetic analysis, analysis in terms of origins, is an obeisance to her and is determined by her kind of consciousness. It is enough to realize that insight can shift perspective from one archetypal background to another and that phenomena now seeming to be of the son can move elsewhere and offer another kind of psychological movement.

VIII

By laying to rest the notion that the puer is only the son of the great mother, we may also abandon former notions of ego-development. Delivery through battle against an overwhelming mother is no longer the only way.[23] The hero of the will—who has been disappearing from

---

23. Jung's classic work *Symbols of Transformation* (*CW* 5) provides a full description

drama and fiction, and political history too (if not from action-packed movies)—is not always a viable role for ego, nor must battle be the way. The dragon demands battle and the hero myth tells us how to proceed. But suppose we were to step out altogether from the great mother, from Jocasta and Oedipus and the exhausting, blinding heroics that so often kill the feminine opposite—not just "out there" in the enemy but within the heroic psyche itself.

If Emerson considered the hero to be he who was immovably centered (which can be reversed to mean he who is so fixed on the center that he has lost his mobility), we might define the hero as he who has maimed femininity. In compensation to this, analytical psychology has long concentrated on the anima as therapy for the ego (or persona) identification. But the basic notions of the anima, and the therapeutic sentimentalisms about her, are in turn the result of the same psychology's efforts to strengthen the ego. The anima would not have to carry feeling, femininity, soul, imagination, introversion, subtlety, and what have you if the ego were not so bound to the hero myth, so fixed in its central focus on "reality," "problems," and "moral choice."[24]

Suppose we were no longer to conceive of the ego's relation to its development and to the spirit on the heroic model, achieving through fighting, keeping in shape, trusting in the right arm, overcoming all darkness with the enlightenment of the ego over the id. Is this the only way to consciousness and culture?

Freud defined the intention of psychoanalysis: "…to strengthen the ego, to make it more independent of the super-ego, to widen its field of perception and enlarge its organization, so that it can appropriate fresh portions of the id. Where id was, there ego shall be. It is a work of culture."[25] Oedipus, hero and king, determines not only the content of psychoanalysis but also its impetus, its heroism. Analysis, psychologi-

---

of the development of consciousness in terms of the hero's struggle with the mother. More or less in the same line are the works of Erich Neumann, *The Origins and History of Consciousness* (New York: Pantheon, 1954), esp. 44–52, and M. Esther Harding, *Psychic Energy: Its Source and Goal*. It is against this background of classic Jungian literature that my critique of the heroic way should be read.

24. See my *Anima: An Anatomy of a Personified Notion* (Putnam, Conn.: Spring Publications, 2007 [1985]).

25. Sigmund Freud, "New Introductory Lectures" in *SE* 22:80.

cal development, becoming conscious are new models of cultural heroism so that the culture hero is the thoroughly analyzed man, sublimated, integrated, whole, conscious. And analysis, as a way of achieving this goal, becomes a suffering pilgrimage or trial by ordeal of the hero. If Freud was right that Oedipus is the stuff of neurosis, then the corollary follows that Oedipus heroics are the dynamism of neurosis.[26] Heroism is thus a kind of neurosis and the heroic ego is neurotic ego. Creative spirit and fertile matter are there embraced and embattled to the destruction of both. Ego-development that is patterned on the hero will have as part of this pattern the shadow of the hero—estrangement from the feminine and compulsive masculinity—foreshadowing the sterile and bitter senex as outcome of the heroic course.

The wandering loneliness of such figures as Jason, Bellerophon, Oedipus (and perhaps Orestes who lived on to seventy) after their great deeds were done, and their failures, may be seen in two different ways. On the one hand, this wandering loneliness is temporal, belonging to the heroic course that issues into the used-up old king. (The hero—was he a puer?—of F. Scott Fitzgerald's *Tender Is the Night* slowly falls away, aimless like Bellerophon, wandering to ever smaller towns through the great plains). But, on the other hand, we may regard synchronically this behavior trait as a senex aspect of the puer from the beginning, his steady companion.

The hero and the puer seem to have to go it alone (unlike Dionysus, who sometimes is the lonely stranger but who is usually together with a crowd). Yes, this characteristic shows something renegade, psychopathic, schizoid; however, if it is a senex attribute within the puer figure, the attempt to socialize a young man who is following a puer pattern violates the style of his individuation and the integration of the senex component. Leave it alone, says the style itself. The socializing impetus is again that of the mother, whereas the spirit does indeed blow in gusts, free, where it will, and often where no one else can go along. For the mother this is hard to take because she is "by nature" everywhere and wants no phase, no part off on its own, unconnected, out of touch. As a myth can be read two ways—strung out into successive events or condensed where all parts are present at any one time—so we may look

---

26. "Oedipus Revisited," in *UE6: Mythic Figures*.

at a life in the same way. Assertive masculinity results in aimlessness, or assertive masculinity results from aimlessness. Owing to the proximity of puer and senex, we cannot tell which comes first.

Assertive masculinity is suspicious. Somewhere we know that it must be reactive to feminine attachment. Mythical levels of the psyche support the suspicion, for there it is recollected that hero and female opponent are inseparable. Although they meet in battle, the hero shouting, they could as well be in bed and groaning, because battle with the mother is a manner of incest. Whether as lover or as enemy, his role is determined by his opposite, his polarity with the mother. When mother determines the role, then regardless how it is played its essence is always the same: son. And, as Jung says of assertive heroism: "Unfortunately, however, this heroic deed has no lasting effects. Again and again the hero must renew the struggle, and always under the symbol of deliverance from the mother...The mother is thus the daemon who challenges the hero to his deeds and lays in his path the poisonous serpent that will strike him."[27] As long as psychotherapy is conceived in terms of ego development, the development will never be strong enough and the task will never be done. Rather than being therapists of psyche, we are therapists (servants and devotees) of mother.

Even the *imitatio Christi*—and especially as it is exhibited in the contemporary program of Christianity in social action—supports the heroic ego and keeps it embroiled in the hassle with the archetypal mother. The "Church in Action" belongs to the myth of the culture hero, a Herculean absorption of Jesus[28] where Jesus fades into the older archetypal patterns of Gilgamesh, Shamash, and Hercules, losing the special relation of Father and Son that Jesus's words themselves so emphasize. Yet Jesus does bring a sword in the heroic fashion, and this blade from the beginning of the Christian era until today is plunged century after century into the body of the dragon, now meaning this, now meaning that, but always consciousness is defined through this slaughter. If in tradi-

---

27. *CW*5, §540.

28. On the Hercules-Christ identifications, see Erwin R. Goodenough, *Jewish Symbols in the Greco-Roman Period* (New York: Pantheon, 1964), 122–23 with notes, and Marcel Simon, *Hercule et le Christianisme* (Paris: Publications de la Faculté des Lettres de l'Université de Strasbourg, 1955); also G. Karl Galinsky, *The Herakles Theme* (Oxford: Blackwell, 1972).

tional Christian heroics the knife slays the evil, in Greek mythic thought the knife *is* the evil.[29] Have we gone far enough when we reflect upon our Western history of incredible bloodshed only in terms of aggression and the aggressive instinct in animals? This takes evil right out of the psyche and puts it safely into some objective field. Let us once look closer at the knife (which animals don't have) and interiorize, psychologize aggression in terms of our very definition of consciousness: the logos sword of discrimination in the hands of the heroic ego in his mission to clean up the mother-benighted world. What we have taken for consciousness, this too has been determined by the mother. To be conscious has meant and continues to mean: to kill.

Discrimination is the essential, the sword only a secondary instrument. Consciousness requires discrimination, for, as Jung said, there is no consciousness without perception of differences. But this perception can use the delicacy of fingers, sensitivity of ear, eye, and taste, a feeling for values and tones and images. There can be puer aesthetic distinctions without swords. The puer has this talent for craft in his background—Joseph the carpenter, Daedalus the inventor;[30] these fathers put the knife to another use.

Hercules is a primordial figure of assertive masculinity and is the killer-culture-hero par excellence. His cult was the most widely observed in Greek antiquity, yet his name means simply Glory of Hera.[31] Although this goddess acts as his enemy before his birth and from his cradle where she sent serpents to kill him, it is this Great Goddess who spurs his deeds as culture hero. In the madness of Hercules described by Euripides, the hero claims he was driven beyond the borders of san-

---

29. Karl Kerényi, "Evil in Greek Mythology can be symbolized by the knife... A man desires to kill if he is 'evil,' and that is the nature of the 'evil'" ("The Problem of Evil in Mythology," in *Evil,* edited by The Curatorium of the C.G. Jung Institute, Zurich [Evanston: Northwestern University Press, 1967], 15ff.)

30. *CW*5, §515.

31. See Philip E. Slater's *The Glory of Hera* (Boston: Beacon, 1971). The book reviews the major Greek mythical figures, especially heroes, and sees them all from within the sociology of the mother-complex, represented by Hera. The gods and heroes he treats are ultimately projections of different styles of the mother-complex. His view is not archetypal; that is, he has not learned from Jung that "...we are obliged to reverse our rationalistic causal sequence, and instead of deriving these figures from our psychic conditions, must derive our psychic conditions from these figures" (*CW*13, §299).

ity into heroic extremes by Hera, who plagued his life throughout. Yet, he is explicitly her servant, even coming to her rescue when she had been accosted by Silenus,[32] and he receives as his bride in final reward Hebe, who is none other than Hera herself in her younger, sweeter, seductive form.

Hercules is merely one of the heroes driven by this Great Goddess to perform his deeds for her civilization. Hera sends the Sphinx to Oedipus; she (Juno) is the specific persecutor of Aeneas and is the background to Jason's exploits. Hera, the tales say, mothered the monster Typhon and nourished the Hydra and Nemean lion. She had a part in the persecutions and slaying of Dionysus. Hera is the "Enemy's consort."[33] Her own children are Ares[34] of the battle-rage and Hephaestus[35] the ironworker, the volcano.

We are so used to assuming that the son of the great mother appears as a beautiful ineffectual who has laid his testicles on her altar and nourishes her soil with his blood, and we are so used to believing that the hero pattern leads away from her, that we have lost sight of the role of the Great Goddess in what is closest to us: our ego-formation. The adapted ego of reality is in her "yoke,"[36] a meaning of Hera, just as the words *hero* and *Hera* are taken by many scholars to be cognate.[37] When

---

32. Karl Kerényi, *The Heroes of the Greeks* (London: Thames and Hudson, 1959), 193.

33. Fontenrose, *Python*, 256–60.

34. For insights on the psychological importance of Ares, see R. Grinnell, "Reflections on the Archetype of Consciousness," *Spring: An Annual of Archetypal Psychology and Jungian Thought* (1970), 25–28; and Whitmont, "On Aggression," 52ff. in the same volume; also Malamud, "The Amazon Problem," 50–52, 54. See also my essay "Wars, Arms, Rams, Mars: On the Love of War," in *Facing Apocalypse*, edited by Valerie Andrews, Robert Bosnak, Karen Walter Goodwin (Thompson, Conn.: Spring Publications, 2021 [1987]).

35. For the psychological importance of Hephaistos, see Murray Stein, "Hephaistos: A Pattern of Introversion," in *Facing the Gods*.

36. W.K.C. Guthrie, *The Greeks and their Gods* (London: Methuen, 1968), 70. The Hera of Argos was called the "goddess of the yoke."

37. Fontenrose, *Python*, 119n.53. Further on the name of Hercules, see Martin P. Nilsson, *The Mycenean Origin of Greek Mythology* (Cambridge: Cambridge University Press, 1932), 189ff. Nilsson, however, misses the psychological point that the opposites are one when he writes that the name of Herakles is clearly composed of Hera and *kles* but finds it "forced and improbable" that Hercules should be called "the fame of

outer life or inner life is conceived as a contest for light, an arena of struggles, success versus failure, coping versus collapse, work versus sleep, pleasure and love, then we are children of Hera.[38] And the ego that results is the mother-complex in a jockstrap.

My point here is to reverse the usual order: puer is weak and mother-bound; hero is strong and mother-free. If the hero is really the strong son whom the mother wants, then we might look at the puer's weaknesses differently.

The son disguises himself as the hyperactive culture hero of civilization, all of whose conquests, glories, triumphs, and spoils ultimately serve the mother of material civilization. The hero of antiquity was so fond of his trophies. Heroic consciousness must have something to show; the ego must have its concrete proof, for such is its definition of reality. Battle has always been for booty and not only for the fun of fighting and pride of winning. But the loot and spoils soon decorate a city, become the furnishings of domestic life, and the hero begins to accumulate possessions—the culture hero as collector. Hero and puer here differ considerably, since the exploits of the former show a preponderance of civilizing virtues, viz., Hercules, Jason, and Theseus. The puer's task is more an odyssey of the spirit, a wandering that never comes home to any hearth or city.

Hera...while this goddess dealt the severest blow to him and imposed pain, grief, and labor upon him."

38. We may read the following description of the hero in the light of psychology's ideals of "ego-strength": "the Homeric hero loved battle, and fighting was his life...A hero's activity...is concentrated on the most testing kind of action, war..." "The hero must use his superior qualities at all times to excel and win applause...He makes honor his paramount code, and glory the driving force and aim of his existence...his ideals are courage, endurance, strength and beauty...he relies upon his own ability to make the fullest use of his powers." "The heroic outlook shook off primitive superstitions and taboos by showing that man can do amazing things by his own effort and by his own nature, indeed that he can almost rise above his own nature." Michael Grant, *Myths of the Greeks and Romans* (New York: Mentor Books, 1962), 45–47. This description covers heroic consciousness as such and not only its extraverted manifestations. The same attitudes and the same battle can take place in the confines of a consulting room, as the heroic attitude wrestles introvertedly with "the unconscious" in order to rise above its own nature.

These considerations of the hero/mother relation must take into account one more essential element in the hero: death. Pointing to any element in heroic psychology as "essential" is always subject to counter-arguments. After all, the hero has been a principal focus for historians of Greek religion and for psychologists, whose writings on this theme reach heroic proportions, as if the theme drives its student into spectacular efforts of mastery. Of the major themes that characterize the hero analyzed and abstracted by Brelich, Farnell, Fontenrose, Kerényi, Nock, Campbell, Harding, Neumann, and Roheim[39] (to extend the list would drive us, too, further into heroics), let us single out *the cult of the burial tumulus* as a central focus of the hero myth. Of course the hero's spectacular mantic and healing powers, his virtue and strength, his cultural deeds, his role as model in initiation and as founder of cult, city, clan, and family should not be overlooked, but most writers agree that the hero cult is bound to a distinct locus and the locus indicated by a burial mound.[40]

When reference is made to a hero in antiquity it is an evocation of something dead; there are no present heroes, no heroes now, living in the present tense. To be a hero (or the hero-in-reverse as antihero) one must be "dead." The hero is dead because he is an imaginal power, a fantasy. The hero is present not in actuality but as a psychic projection through his cult, in his local tumulus where he is buried, and only "after" the events and through legends of them. The hero himself has

---

39. Angelo Brelich, *Gli eroeci* (Rome: Ediziono dell'Ateneo, 1958); Lewis Richard Farnell, *Greek Hero Cults and Ideas of Immortality* (Oxford: The Clarendon Press, 1921); Fontenrose, *Python*, op. cit.; Kerényi, *The Heroes of the Greeks*, op. cit.; A.D. Nock, "The Cult of Heroes," *Harvard Theological Review* 37 (1944); Joseph Campbell, *The Hero with a Thousand Faces* (New York: Pantheon Books, 1949); M. Esther Harding, "The Inner Conflict: The Dragon and the Hero," in *Psychic Energy*, op. cit.; Neumann, *The Origins and History of Consciousness*, op. cit.; Géza Róheim, "The Dragon and the Hero," *American Imago* 1, no. 3 (1940). This list is by no means intended to be complete, especially as it does not extend into the area of heroic literature (epic) or the hero in various sorts of fiction, nor does it refer to the hero figure in nonclassical accounts, e.g., fairytale and folklore and in exotic cultures, etc. For a comparative study of the hero in poetry and the heroic style, see C.M. Bowra's massive opus *Heroic Poetry* (London: Macmillan, 1961).

40. For more on the underworld affiliations of the hero, see my *The Dream and the Underworld* (New York: Harper & Row, 1979), 110ff.

been translated to the Isles of the Blest, removed, distant, out of it. The hero is a revenant, providing a fantasy for what the complex can do with itself. The hero gives us the model for that peculiar process upon which our civilization rests: dissociation. We worship the drive of the complex and refuse its inertia. The inertia we call unconscious, regressive, dragon, mother; the drive we call consciousness. We all, whose "family" and "city" are founded upon heroic consciousness and whose initiation is modeled upon the hero, are haunted by this revenant spirit that takes the basic element of psychic life, the complex, from one side only, the negentropic upward direction, calling the dynamic movement it releases "ego." In this manner the complex civilizes itself through achievements, casting off its inertia into unconsciousness. The heroic presents forward marching spirit, active in its questing and transcendent to life (dead) and in the Isles of the Blest.[41] These characteristics may also occur (as we set out in other chapters) as puer themes. Therefore, the puer can be readily caught up in heroics. But there is a difference, and this difference may be conceived in regard to death, the element we have considered central to the idea of the hero.

The son, the hero, and the puer may all die the same death. But I would hazard a suggestion about differences: the son's "death" is for the mother (Attis, say); the hero's "death" is because of the mother (Hercules and Hera, Baldur and Frigg, Achilles and Thetis[42]); the puer's death is independent of the mother. These distinctions are again one of attitude, perspective, not of mythical "fact," and bespeak the place that death holds within the psyche for son, hero, and puer. Where death means sac-

---

41. Frequently, the hero is translated to the Isles of the Blest without "dying." He simply "leaves the scene," because a god favors him, and is removed into isolation (Cf. Erwin Rohde, *Psyche*, 8th ed. [London: Routledge, 1925], 64–76). Often it is the mother who raises the hero to immortality—Phaethon by Aphrodite, Telegonos by Circe, Achilles by Thetis, Memnon by Eos, but Hercules from his flaming funeral pyre was borne aloft by Zeus. The Isles of the Blest are ruled over by Kronos (the senex), so that even in this mythologem there recurs the motif of the reunion with the senex, the mother being in these cases the detour (through heroism) and then the necessary helper.

42. The overt cause of Achilles's death is Apollo (or Paris), but the spot hit is the heel, that place where Thetis held Achilles while dipping him into invulnerability. His ultimate cause of death was precisely where she had touched and held him to keep him safe.

rifice (the son) or victory (hero)—"death, where is thy sting"—the mother is playing her significant role. Death connected with the senex, its survival, its depression, its penetrating insight, presents another image and emotion.

IX

Son and Great Mother metamorphose into hero and serpent—or do they? Jung says that the hero and the dragon he overcomes are brothers or even one; the man who has power over the daemonic is himself touched by the daemonic.[43] Harrison wrote that the snake as *daimon* is the double of the hero; the early hero had snake form, and even the higher gods (Ares, Apollo, Hermes, Zeus) have their serpent aspect as did Demeter and Athene.[44] If hero and serpent are one, then the battle turns the hero against his own nature. But what precisely does he turn against, and how does the animal double of his own structure, this *daimon* or dragon or serpent, become "mother"? Psychology's approach to this motif is usually in terms of development. "Development" has been the master-key to all the locked riddles in modern psychology, just as "fertility" once opened what we did not understand in mythology and archeology. The supposed development of consciousness occurs from a darker level to a lighter one, from only matter to also spirit, from only

43. *CW*5,§§575, 580, 593, 671; cf. Harding, *Psychic Energy*, 259ff. Harding makes the hero-dragon issue excessively moral, as if she were in a Christian version of that myth herself, saying of the kinship between dragon and dragon slayer: "The renegade in man is closely related in its nature to the slothful aspect of the dragon, while the forward-going, heroic element in him is more nearly related to the energy of the dragon. Thus the human being who has conquered the dragon and assimilated its power through tasting its blood or eating its heart becomes a superman." If dragon be translated into "the unconscious," what high hopes, what Nietzschean hopes, analysis bodes the striving ego! If dragon be translated into "imagination" or "vitality" or "Mercurius," what devastation!

44. On the snake forms of the gods and heroes, see J. Harrison, *Themis*, section on "Daimon and Hero"; Erich Küster, *Die Schlange in der griechischen Kunst und Religion* (Giessen: A. Töpelmann, 1913); Fontenrose, *Python*, passim. Artemidorus (*Oneirocriticus* 1.13) said that the "snake is the symbol of all gods to whom it is sacred, viz. Zeus, Sabazius, Helios, Demeter, Core, Hecate, Asclepius, and the Heroes." On Apollo and snake, Karl Kerényi, "Apollonian Epiphanies," in his *Apollo: The Wind, the Spirit, and the God: Four Studies*, translated by Jon Solomon (Dallas: Spring Publications, 1983), 21–45.

nature to also culture. This "development of consciousness" supposedly occurs historically in civilizations, phylogenetically in the species and race, and ontogenetically in each individual from maternal attachment to paternal self-reliance. The hero against serpent is thus the *paradigm* for the kernel structure in our personal and collective consciousness.

Were we to be interviewed by an aboriginal anthropologist from Australia for our "dream," our "gods," and our "cosmology," this would be the story we would tell. We would tell of the struggle each day brings to Ego who must rise and do battle with Depression and Seduction and Entanglement, so as to keep the world safe from Chaos, Evil, and Regression, which coil round it like an oppressive Swallowing Serpent. This gives account to our inquirer of our peculiar irrationalities: why we sweep the streets, why we pay taxes, why we go to school and to war—all with compulsive ritualistic energy so as to keep the Serpent at bay. This is our true cosmology; for Ego, who changes rivers in their course and shoots to the moon, acts not out of hunger or gods or tribal persecutions, as the inquiring aboriginal might imagine in his savage mind, so inert and lazy, bound to the maternal uroboros, with his "weak ego." No, our civilization's excessive activism is all to keep back the night of the Serpent, requiring a single monotheistic single-mindedness, a cyclop's dynamism of all the gods that She and Ego have partaken in together at a Western banquet lasting three thousand years and perhaps now coming to its indigestible conclusion as Ego weakens in what we call "neurosis" and the swallowed gods stir again in the imaginal dark of his shadow and of her belly. Ego and Unconscious, Hero and Serpent, Son and Mother, their battle, their bed and their banquet—this is the sustaining myth we must tell to account for our strange ways: why we are always at war, why we have eaten up the world, why we have so little imaginative power, and why we have only one God and He so far away.

Snake and dragon are *not* one and the same. The snake is a piece of nature and well represents instinctual being, especially the hard-to-grasp movements of introverting libido. But the dragon does not exist in external nature. It is a fantasy instinct, or the instinct of fantasy, which the hero slays, thereby becoming the single-minded ego of will-power. If the snake is the daimon of the instinctual psyche, the dragon, who shoots fire from his tongue and eyes, blazes with color, and controls the waters, who lives below our daily world but could as well with his wings inhabit the sky, is the *daimon* of our imaginal psyche. The masculine sword of reason in the masculine hand of will kills both snake and dragon, both instinct and imagination in daily combat as Ego enacts our central myth.

Undoubtedly, the dragon has moon associations; and the snake has feminine connotations in mythological and in psychological material and can be found in our culture in association with the Great Goddess. But the snake can as well be found with heroes, kings, and gods. It is strongly sexual, phallic even, yet transcends gender. It appears in the religion of primordial man. (Adam, too, has his snake.) Like nature, instinct, libido, or the *mercurius* of alchemy—for each of which the serpent stands—it is a primordial form of life, or life in its primordiality, *Ur*-life. *The serpent is primordiality itself,* which can transform into anything, so that we experience it in sexuality, project it backward into ancestors as their ghost, envision it in earth or below it, hear its wisdom, fear its death.[45] It is a power, a numinosity, a primordiality of religion. Its meanings renew with its skin and peel off as we try to grasp hold. (The dragon's many heads say we cannot meet it with one idea alone.) The slippery flow of meanings makes it possible for Great Goddess and daimon to merge, to lose their distinction, so that by means of the serpent (Hera sending the snakes to baby Hercules) the mother gets at the puer and brings his fall into heroism. She tempts him into the fight for deliverance from her. By falling for the challenge he is delivered of his own daimon. Like Beowulf he dies when he kills the dragon. The Dragon-Fight is his undoing.

In the mixture of the three components—man, mother, snake—the snake loses its life, the man loses his snake, but the mother has her hero. This leaves him without wisdom, without chthonic depths, vital imagination, or phallic consciousness, a one-sided solar-hero for a civilization ruled by the mother or by the senex whose snakes have gone into the sewers. By losing chthonic consciousness, which means his psychoid *daimon* root that trails into the ancestors in Hades, he loses his root in death, becoming the real victim of the "Battle for Deliverance,"[46] and

---

45. Cf. "A Snake is not a Symbol" in James Hillman and Margot McLean, *Dream Animals* (San Francisco: Chronicle Books, 1997), 25–29.

46. *CW*5, Part 2, chap. 6.

ready for Hebe. Because the heroic way to spirit goes against the snake, it is secretly a self-destruction.

By turning against the snake, heroic consciousness also tends to lose the other animals of the mother world, especially the cow of nature. With this goes the warmth, the muzzle and the eyes, the rumination and the slowness, the pastures for the soul, Hera as Hathor, the holiness of life and its rhythm. In the struggle for independence and self-reliance, he can no longer return to the stable without fearing decomposition. (Hercules cleans stables.) So, of course, heroic consciousness cannot get through, as fairy tales say, without the helpful animal. A consciousness that had not defined itself by refusing the animal in the first place would not be in this predicament of lost animal help, its sureness and knowledge of survival.

Furthermore, heroic consciousness constellates its fundamental opposite as feminine and as enemy. The great figures on whose patterns we build our ego strength—Oedipus and Hercules, Achilles, Hippolytus, and Orpheus—in different ways opposed the feminine and fell victim to it. Could we not turn another way? Could we become conscious without that struggle? Ego development has so long been conceived through the heroics of tough aggression, paranoid misogyny, selfishness, and distance of feeling so typical of the mother's son that we have neglected other paths opened by the puer.

Must the feminine continue to be the primary enemy to be magnified into a *magna mater* whom one succumbs to, worships, or battles, but with whom one never simply pairs as equal though different? Whenever we are sons of this Great Feminine, the feminine is experienced as "great." Woman is idealized. She is endowed with the divine power to save or destroy. We look for the wonderful woman to be our salvation, which then constellates the other side, betrayal and destruction. Every idealization of the feminine is only a propitiation of her other components: the Amazons, the Furies, the Graeae, the Sirens, the Harpies, Circe, Phaedra, Medea, Baubo, Persephone, Hecate, Gorgo, Medusa. The expectation to be saved by a woman goes hand in hand with the fear of being destroyed by her.

Here we come upon one more difference between puer and heroic son. The magnification of the mother-complex is a sure sign that we are choosing the heroic role whose purpose is less spirit and less psyche than it is the traditional ego, its strengthening and its development. The epic dramas in which the hero is cast with impossible tasks, miraculous weapons, overwhelming enemies, and where mother is a dragon, witch, or goddess can well make a man forget the ordinary mother in the case. But in many tales the mother is merely human, or a lowly nymph, reminding consciousness of its commonness. By keeping to this personal, ordinary, human mother, her specific pathological lacks and her unique graces, we can keep at our backs as support the sense of human ordinariness given by the limits of our *actual personal mother* complex, what she passes to us and how we descend from her, for which we have gratitude. She is our history, and it is from her simple lap that we fell (*casus*) as a case. By keeping her in proportion, we can then reserve the *magnificatio* for the puer archetype itself, its narcissism and high-flying ambition to create. The hero's *hybris* (inflation) arises from his hidden identity with the mother; the puer's *superbia* (arrogance) reflects his cocky, narcissistic conviction that he is about his father's business, a child of the spirit, bearing its message.

Released from these mystiques of the son-great mother, the feminine could show other individualities, as in the *Odyssey*. There the feminine plays many roles: Goddess (Athene), Mistress (Calypso), Devourer (Scylla and Charybdis), Enchantress (Circe), Mother-Daughter (Arete-Nausicaa), Personal Mother (Anticlea), Rescuer (Ino), Seductress (Sirens), Nurse (Eurycleia), and Wife (Penelope).[47] With each, man

---

47. See W.B. Stanford, chap. 4: "Personal Relationships," in his *The Odysseus Theme: A Study in the Adaptability of a Traditional Hero* (Thompson: Conn.: Spring Publications, 2022 [1954]). In contrast with Odysseus, let us review the relation to feminine figures in certain other Greek heroes. Oedipus belonged to the race Spartoi, "Dragon people," supposedly a matriarchy without paternal principle. He did not recognize his own father because "the child does not know his own begetter, and this is what makes patricide possible" (J.J. Bachofen, *Myth, Religion, and Mother Right*, translated by Ralph Manheim [Princeton, N.J.: Princeton University Press, 1967], 180–81). As Oedipus is conceived in the line of the Dragons, so is he inconceivable without that complementary mother/dragon, first as Sphinx (sent by Hera, or her fantasy), then as Jocasta. Hercules's relation with women is summed up by Bachofen (176): "It is characteristic that Hercules alone of all the heroes remained on board the Argo and reproached his friends for lying with the Amazons...In all his myths he is the irreconcilable foe of matriarchy, the indefatigable battler of Amazons, the misogynist, in whose sacrifice no woman takes part, by whose name no woman swears, and who finally meets

finds individual ways of coming to terms, loving and being furthered. There, the feminine does not threaten the eventual rapprochement of father and son. (But Odysseus, like the King figure in alchemy, is himself *senex-et-puer.*) The feminine in the Odyssey works throughout for the reunion of the divided house of Ithaca, giving us a model for the way in which feminine patterns can weave together puer and senex, rather than divide them further through the penchant of the great mother for heroics that magnify her into a man's main concern, literalizing his psychic reality, clouding his puer vision, and distracting him away from his puer necessities.

---

his death from a woman's poisoned garment." Achilles, of the Greek heroes at Troy, was the only one who was a son of a goddess (Kerényi, *Heroes,* 347) and was finally overcome by an arrow of Paris, the favorite of Aphrodite and the paramour of Helen. Although a most unheroic and unmilitaristic figure, Paris of "the soft weak ways" (Rachel Bespaloff, *On the Iliad* [New York: Pantheon, 1947], 64) is the one who overcomes Achilles. Paris is the Achilles's heel of the hero. Hippolytus was slain through the revenge of Aphrodite whom he had spurned. Orpheus, as Vergil and Ovid describe him, shunned entirely the company of women after he had lost Eurydice—or did his misogyny result in her loss to the serpent's bite? (W.K.C. Guthrie, *Orpheus and Greek Religion* [London: Methuen, 1952], 31). He let no women in his cult; and thus "in the established tradition it is the women of Thrace who make him their victim" (ibid., 32). Aeschylus, who is the earliest source for the legend of his death, presents the Maenads of Dionysus as his slayers. But, as Guthrie points out (ibid., 33), other legends tell it differently: the women themselves excluded by Orphic misogyny took their revenge. Furthermore, earlier evidence of vase paintings shows him not torn to pieces (maenad-style), but speared and hacked and stoned by women in a melée of feminine wrath rather than in a Dionysian ritual. However we view it, the point remains: feminine figures were his enemy and did him in. Achilles's son Neoptolemus ("renewer of war"), also called Pyrrhus ("redhead") (Marie Delcourt, *Pyrrhos et Pyrrha: Recherches sur les valeurs du jeu dans les légendes helléniques* [Paris: Société d'Édition "Les Belles Lettres," 1965], ch. 2), is the one who murders Priam of Troy and the boy infant who would have been the carrier of its line (Euripides, *Trojan Women*). "Vase paintings often combine the death of the old king and that of his grandson at the hands of Neoptolemo" (Margaret R. Scherrer, *The Legends of Troy* [London: Phaidon, 1964], 123). This renewer of Achilles's spirit is the murderer of a senex-puer pair, and he follows the heroic pattern by meeting death at the hands of women: either at the instigation of the Pythian priestess or in the form of a Pyrrhus, King of Epirus, killed by a woman who hurls a tile at him from a rooftop. What comes first: killed by a woman, his woman-killer nature, or his killing the senex-puer pair? Contrast Odysseus!

X

If I could sum up into one main thought the many ideas we have touched upon, it would be this. Jung makes a clear distinction between the role of the mother archetype as regressive and devouring, on the one hand, and as the creative matrix, on the other. He places this duality within the fantasy of another duality—the first and second halves of life. For young consciousness "entry into the mother" is a fatal incest; for old consciousness it is the way of renewal and even that which he calls the way of individuation.[48] We can free this important idea of Jung's from the frame of its presentation. First and second half, young and old, are another way of putting the puer-senex duality. They are structures of consciousness valid *always* and not only as they are divided from each other into first and second halves of life. Because our culture appears now to be in a period when its heroic ego has peaked and where the senex dominant, and so the puer complement, is now of extreme relevance, collective consciousness itself is in what Jung would call "the second half." For anyone in this culture at this time the battle with the mother and the heroic stance of the "first half" cannot but be archetypally wrong, regardless of one's age. This stance is anachronistic in the true sense of being out of tune with time, and every victory over the mother is a defeat for the fundamental task of the present culture: becoming aware of the senex in all its archetypal significance, relating puer phenomena to it, and releasing puer possibilities within it.

---

48. *CW*5, §459.

The Moon and Matriarchal Consciousness

ERICH NEUMANN

In the history of the beginnings of consciousness we can discern successive phases of development during which the ego frees itself from
containment in the unconscious, the original uroboric situation, and
finally, at the end of the process, having become the center of modern Western consciousness, confronts the unconscious as a separated
system in the psyche. During this development, leading to a liberation
from the ascendancy of the unconscious, the symbolism of consciousness is masculine and that of the unconscious, insofar as it stands in
opposition to the emancipation of the ego, is feminine, as we learn from
mythology and the symbolism of the collective unconscious.

The phase in which ego-consciousness is still childlike, that is,
dependent in its relation to the unconscious, is represented in myth by
the archetype of the Great Mother. The constellation of this psychic situation, as well as of its forms of expression and projection, we have termed
"matriarchy," and, in contradistinction to this, we will speak of the tendency of the ego to free itself from the unconscious, and to dominate it,
as the "patriarchal accent" in the development of consciousness.

Therefore, matriarchy and patriarchy are psychic stages that are
characterized by different developments of the conscious and the
unconscious, and especially by different attitudes of the one toward the

Originally published in *Eranos Yearbook* 18 (1950) as "Der Mond und das matriar-
chale Bewusstsein." The English translation by Hildegard Nagel is an abbreviated
adaption made at the suggestion of the author, first published in *Spring: Contribu-
tions to Jungian Thought* (1954).

other. Matriarchy not only signifies the dominance of the Great Mother archetype, but, in a general way, a total psychic situation in which the unconscious (and the feminine) are dominant, and consciousness (and the masculine) have not yet reached self-reliance and independence. ("Masculine" and "feminine" are here symbolic magnitudes, not to be identified with the "man" or the "woman" as carriers of specific sexual characteristics.) In this sense, a psychological stage, a religion, a neurosis, and also a stage in the development of consciousness, can be called "matriarchal," and "patriarchal" does not mean the sociological rule of men, but the dominance of a masculine consciousness that succeeds in separating the systems of consciousness and unconsciousness and is relatively firmly established in a position opposite to, and independent of, the unconscious. For this reason, modern woman must also go through all those developments that lead to the formation of the patriarchal consciousness that is now typical of, and taken for granted in, the Western conscious situation, being dominant in patriarchal culture.

However, along with this "patriarchal consciousness" exists a "matriarchal consciousness" whose effectiveness is hidden but significant. "Matriarchal consciousness" belongs to the matriarchal layer of the psyche that shaped civilization in the early period of human history. It characterizes the spiritual nature of woman—apart from the cultural contribution of woman to patriarchal consciousness—but it also plays an important role in the life of man. Wherever consciousness is not liberated in a patriarchal way from the unconscious, "matriarchal consciousness" dominates: that is, in the early days of humanity and, ontogenetically, in the corresponding phases of childhood; likewise, in the man in whom occurs an accentuated activity on the part of the anima, the feminine side of his psychology, in psychological crises, as well as in creative processes.

Before seeking to reach a deeper psychological understanding of matriarchal consciousness, let us indulge in an "etymological intermezzo on the moon," which will tell us something about the structure of the moon archetype. We will find that the psychological aspect of the archetype may provide an inner, central point of relationship between roots that have hitherto been considered as having no linguistic connection.

Etymology[1] has attempted to separate two roots: on the one hand, the moon-root, which with *men* (moon) and *mensis* (month) belongs to the root *ma* and the Sanscrit root *mās*, and on the other, the Sanscrit root *manas*, with *menos* (Greek), *mens* (Latin), etc., which represents the spirit *par excellence.*

From the spirit-root stems a wide ramification of significant spiritual meanings: *menos*, spirit, heart, soul, courage, ardency; *menoinan*, to consider, meditate, wish; *memona*, to have in mind, to intend; *mainomai*, to think, but also to be lost in thoughts and to rave, with which belongs *mania*, madness, possession, and also *manteia*, prophecy. Other branches of the same spirit-stem are *menis*, *menos*, anger; *menuō*, indicate, reveal; *menō*, remain, linger; *manthanō*, to learn; *memini*, to remember; and *mentiri*, to lie. All these spirit-roots stem from the one original Sanscrit root *mati-h*, which means thought, intention.

On no grounds whatever, this root has been set in opposition to the moon-root, *men*, moon; *mensis*, month; *mās*, which is connected with *ma*, to measure. From it stems not only *matra-m*, measure, but also *metis*, cleverness, wisdom; *metiesthai*, to meditate, to have in mind, to dream; and, moreover, to our surprise we ascertain that this moon-root, purportedly opposed to the spirit-root, is likewise derived from the Sanscrit root *mati-h*, meaning measure, knowing.[2]

Hence, the single archetypal root underlying these meanings is the moon-spirit, which expresses itself in all of the diversified branchings, thus revealing to us its nature and its primal meaning. What emanates from the moon-spirit is an emotional movement closely related to the activities of the unconscious. In active eruption it is a fiery spirit—it is courage, anger, possession, and rage; its self-revelation leads to prophecy, cogitation, and lying, but also to poetry. Along with this fiery productivity, however, goes another, more "measured" attitude that meditates, dreams, waits and wishes, hesitates and lingers, which is related to memory and learning, and whose outcome is moderation, wisdom, and meaning.

---

1. Cf. the following etymological dictionaries: J. and W. Grimm, *Deutsches Wörterbuch*; E. Littré, *Dictionnaire de la langue française*; E. Boisacq, *Dictionnaire etymologique de la langue grecque.*

2. Boisacq, *Dictionnaire de la langue grecque.*

In discussing this subject elsewhere,[3] I mentioned, as a primary activity of the unconscious, the *Einfall,* that is, the hunch or thought that "pops" into the head. The appearance of spiritual contents that thrust themselves into consciousness with sufficient convincing force to fascinate and control it, probably represents the first form of the emergence of the spirit in man. While, with an expanded consciousness and a stronger ego, this emerging factor is introjected and thought of as an inner psychic manifestation, in the beginning it appears to approach the psyche from "outside" as a sacred revelation and a numinous message from the "powers" or gods. The ego, experiencing these contents as arriving from without, even when it calls them intuitions or inspirations, meets the spontaneous spiritual phenomenon with the attitude characteristic of the ego of matriarchal consciousness. For it is still as true as ever that the revelations of the moon-spirit are more easily received when night animates the unconscious and brings introversion, than in the bright light of day.

Naturally, matriarchal consciousness is not confined to women; it exists also in men, insofar as their consciousness is an anima-consciousness. This is particularly true of creative people; yet the consciousness of everyone depends upon the activity of the unconscious for inspiration and "hunch," as well as for the functioning of instincts, and the "provision of libido" for consciousness. All these things are ruled by the moon, and therefore require a harmony with the moon, an adjustment to it; that is, a moon-cult.

Of prime significance in the moon-cult is the role of the moon as measurer of time. But moon-time is not the abstract, quantitative time of scientific, patriarchal consciousness. It is qualitative time; it changes, and in changing assumes different qualities. Moon-time has periods and rhythms, it waxes and wanes, is favorable or unfavorable. As the time that rules the cosmos, it also rules the earth, and all things that live, and the feminine.

The waxing moon is more than a measurer of time. It is a symbol, like the waning moon, the full moon, and the dark moon, for an inner and outer quality of life and humanity. We can most clearly represent to ourselves the archetypal character of the moon's periods by the changing

---

3. See the untranslated Part I of this article in *Eranos Yearbook* 18.

force of their radiations. For they are centers of the waves of vibration, the streams of power, which, from within and without, pulse through the world and permeate psycho-biological life. Moon-time conditions human living too. New moon and full moon were the earliest sacred times; the dark of the moon, as the victory of the dark night dragon, was the first typical time of darkness and evil. Moreover, seeding and harvest, growth and ripeness, the success and the failure of every enterprise and action, were also dependent on the constellation of cosmic moon-time.

It is, of course, in the feminine that the nature and periodicity of the moon are particularly manifested, and therefore the masculine mind continues to identify the feminine with the moon. Not only is the feminine physically bound to the moon by the monthly change (though no longer dependent on the outer moon period), but the whole of feminine "mentality" is determined by the moon, and its form of spirituality is impressed upon it by the moon archetype, as the epitome of matriarchal consciousness.

The periodicity of the moon, with its nocturnal background, is the symbol of a spirit that waxes and wanes, conforming to the dark processes of the unconscious. Moon-consciousness, as matriarchal consciousness might be called, is never divorced from the unconscious, for it is a phase, a spiritual phase, of the unconscious itself. The ego of matriarchal consciousness possesses no free, independent activity of its own; it waits passively, attuned to the spirit-impulse carried toward it by the unconscious.

A time is "favorable" or "unfavorable" according to whether the spiritual activity determined by the unconscious turns toward the ego and reveals itself, or turns away, darkens, and disappears. At this stage of matriarchal consciousness, the ego's task is to wait and watch for the favorable or unfavorable time, to put itself in harmony with the changing moon, to bring about a consonance, a unison with the rhythm of its emanations.

In other words, matriarchal consciousness is dependent upon mood, upon harmony with the unconscious. This moon-dependency can be viewed as instability or caprice, yet, on the other hand, it provides a backdrop that acts like a sounding board, endowing matriarchal consciousness with a special and positive character. Its response to the rhythm, the times and tides of waxing and waning, of crescendo and decrescendo, give it something of the quality of music. Therefore, music and dance, because of their accented rhythm, play an important role in creating and activating matriarchal consciousness, and in establishing a consonance between the ego and femininity and its ruler, the moon-spirit.[4]

A musical character of an intoxicating orgiastic nature appertains to the deepest involvements and greatest heights of feminine being. Here, as in music, an emotion driving toward disintegration, and a simultaneous, irrational experience of harmony combine together, according to an inner, invisible law. The source of seduction and transport ranges from the *fascinans*[5] of a singing voice, or the Pied Piper's flute, to the ecstatic music of the Dionysian mysteries, the dissolving power of music in orgiastic ritual, and the effect of music on modern woman.[6]

The connection between time, the unconscious, and the moon-spirit belongs, even more profoundly than has so far been shown, to the essential nature of matriarchal consciousness; and it is only by an adequate grasp of the spirit-character of the moon-archetype that we can understand the meaning of matriarchal consciousness and of "feminine spirit."

------

4. It is not an accident that the sphere of the muses, that is, of the feminine powers who preside over music, rhythm, dance, soothsaying, and everything artistically creative, is associated through the numbers three and nine with the moon. (Cf. Karl Kerényi, "Die orphische Kosmogonie und der Ursprung der Orphik," *Eranos Yearbook* 17 (1949). Similarly, it is the figures of Musaios, of his son Eumolpos, and of Orpheus (see J. J. Bachofen, *Das Mutterrecht*, Part 2, in *Gesammelte Werke*, vol. 3 [Basel: Benno Schwabe, 1948], 849, 856 ff.) that become so especially important for the traditions of matriarchal consciousness in the Orphic and Eleusinian mysteries. A further example is that in China the origin of the theater was ascribed to the moon. An emperor who visited the moon, as the legend relates, was so enchanted by the singing and dancing fairies that on his return to earth he instructed some youths to make a terrestrial copy of their songs and postures, and so created the beginning of the Chinese theater; Juliet Bredon and Igor Mitrophanow, *Das Mondjahr: Chinesische Sitten, Bräuche und Feste* (Berlin: Paul Zsolnay Verlag, 1937), 420.

5. See Rudolf Otto, *The Idea of the Holy*, translated by John W. Harvey (London: Oxford University Press, 1929), xv and ch. 4: "The Element of Fascination."

6. Music is not only the specific art of the temporal, but of moon-symbolism as a whole; the concept of qualitative time, of rhythm, of phases, etc., determines its fundamental structure—and by no means only in primitive music.

The way in which an idea, an inspiration, or an intoxication aris-
ing from the unconscious seizes a personality as if by a sudden, violent
assault, driving it to ecstasy, insanity, poetry, or prophecy, represents
one part of the spirit's working. The corresponding trait of matriarchal consciousness is its dependence for every intuition and inspiration upon what emerges from the unconscious, mysteriously and almost
beyond influence, when, where, and how it will. From this point of view,
all shamanism, including prophecy, is a passive sufferance; its activity is more that of "conceiving" than of a willed act; and the essential
contribution of the ego consists in a readiness to accept the emerging
unconscious content and come into harmony with it. Since, however,
this independence of consciousness is characteristic of the autonomous emergence of all unconscious contents, the moon very frequently
appears as the symbol of the unconscious in general.

The relation between time and the moon in matriarchal consciousness, the moon's lordship of time, becomes clear to us only when we
pursue the time significance of the moon beyond the cosmic-mytholog-
ical realm into its effect on the psychology of the individual.

The development of patriarchal consciousness culminates in a relative liberation and independence from the unconscious that leaves the
ego in command of a differentiated system of consciousness with a certain amount of disposable libido, libido that can be applied at will. We
must understand the importance of this patriarchal form of consciousness, even while rejecting the self-deception that makes it interpret
itself as an absolutely free system. Masculine patriarchal consciousness, as shown by the development of the species man, is a highly practical and effective organ of adaptation and accomplishment. Among its
advantages are its constant readiness to react and the extraordinary
swiftness of its reactions and adaptations; for although instinctual reactions guided by the sense organs are prompt indeed, the speed that the
consciousness of modern man has achieved by specialization fa: outstrips them. This speeding up of conscious reactions is brought about
by the same processes that led to the detachment of patriarchal consciousness from the unconscious.[7] As a final development, we see processes of abstraction, which assist in the free disposal and application

---

7. Erich Neumann, *The Origins and History of Consciousness*, translated by R.F.C.
Hull (New York: Pantheon Books, 1954).

of ideas and, in the differentiated thinking type, lead to the manipulation of abstractions, like numbers in mathematics and concepts in logic. In the psychological sense such abstractions are in the highest degree without emotional content.

While patriarchal consciousness annihilates time and outstrips nature's slow processes of transformation and evolution by its purposive use of experiment and calculation, matriarchal consciousness remains caught in the spell of the changing moon. Like the moon, its illumination and its luminosity are bound to. the flow of time and to periodicity. It must wait for time to ripen, while with time, like sown seed, comprehension ripens too.

In ritual and cult, waiting and awaiting are identical with encirclement, with circumambulation. In the wonderful story told by the Brothers Grimm about the nixie in the mill pond,[8] as well as in many other fairy tales, the woman must wait until the moon is full again. Till then she must continue circling the lake in silence, or she must spin her spool full. Only when the time is "fulfilled" does understanding come as an illumination. Similarly, in woman's primal mysteries, in boiling, baking, fermenting, and roasting, the ripening and "getting done," the transformation, is always connected with a period of waiting. The ego of matriarchal consciousness is used to keeping still until the time is favorable, until the process is complete, until the fruit of the moon-tree has ripened into a full moon; that is, until comprehension has been born out of the unconscious. For the moon is not only lord of growth, but also, as moon-tree and life-tree, always itself a growth, "the fruit that begets itself."

It is in the act of "understanding" that the peculiar and specific difference between the processes of matriarchal and patriarchal consciousness first becomes apparent. For matriarchal consciousness, understanding is not an act of the intellect, functioning as an organ for swift registration, development and organization;[9] rather, it has

8. *Grimms' Fairy Tales,* translated by Margaret Hunt and James Stern (New York: Pantheon Books, 1944), 736.

9. Here, and in the following, thinking is taken only as the clearest example of a differentiated function, whose dominance is characteristic of patriarchal consciousness; see C.G. Jung, *Psychological Types,* translated by H.G. Baynes (New York: Harcourt Brace & Co., 1926), 611, and Neumann, *Origins and History of Consciousness.*

the meaning of a "conception." Whatever is to be understood must first "enter" matriarchal consciousness in the full, sexual, symbolic meaning of a fructification.

But this feminine symbolism does not stop here, for that which has entered must "come forth." The phrase "to come forth" marvelously expresses the double aspect of matriarchal consciousness, which experiences the light of consciousness like seed that has sprouted. But when something enters and then even comes forth again, this "something" involves the whole psyche, which is now permeated through and through with the full-grown perception that it must realize, must make real, with its full self. This means that the conceiving and understanding have brought about a personality change. The new content has seized and stirred the whole being, whereas in patriarchal consciousness it would too often only have been filed in one intellectual pigeon-hole or another. Just as a patriarchal consciousness finds it difficult to realize fully and not merely meet with "superb" understanding, so a matriarchal consciousness finds it difficult to understand without first "realizing." And here, to realize means to "bear," to bring to birth; it means submitting to a mutual relation and interaction like that of the mother and the embryo in pregnancy.

Matriarchal qualitative time is always a unique and single occurrence, like a pregnancy, in contrast to the quantitative time of patriarchal consciousness. For, to patriarchal ego-consciousness, every section of time is equal; but matriarchal consciousness has learned, from the timing of the moon, to know the individuality of cosmic time, if not yet that of the ego. The uniqueness and indestructibility of time are constellated for the eye of one schooled to perceive the growth of living things, able to experience and realize the pregnancy of a moment, its readiness for birth. A fairy tale relates that once in a hundred years, on a certain day, at a definite hour, a treasure rises from the deep and will belong to him who finds it at this right moment of its growth.[10] Only a matriarchal consciousness, adjusted to the processes of the unconscious, can recognize the individual time element; a patriarchal consciousness, to which this is one of innumerable, similar moments, will necessarily miss it. In this respect, the matriarchal consciousness is

---

10. Characteristically, it is often said that the treasure "blooms."

more concrete and closer to actual life, while the patriarchal is more abstract and further from reality.

Therefore, the language of symbolism would, as a rule, situate matriarchal consciousness not in the head, but in the heart. Here, understanding means also an act of inclusive feeling and very often this act—as, for instance, in creative work—has to be accompanied by the most intense affect-participation, if anything is to shine forth and illuminate. The abstract thought of patriarchal consciousness is "cold" in comparison, for the objectivity demanded of it presupposes an aloofness possible only to cold blood and a cool head.

Moon-consciousness has been generally associated with the heart by all peoples for whom the head has not yet become the center of a patriarchal consciousness detached from the unconscious. In Egypt, the heart was believed to be the original source of thought and of the creative spirit, and in India, where it was cosmically associated with the moon, the heart was held to be the seat of the *manas,* another word belonging to the root *men,* signifying a psychical organ of the spirit, and so became the place of manifestation for the highest divinity. This heart-center of matriarchal consciousness, with its relation to moon-time, is still the valid orientating factor in all processes of growth and transformation. Its dominance is also typical of the processes of the creative spirit, in the course of which contents are slowly constellated in the unconscious, more or less independent of conscious participation, until they flow up into a consciousness that is neither systematized nor insulated, but open and ready to expand.

That the seat of matriarchal consciousness is in the heart and not the head means—to point out only one implication of the symbolism—that the ego of patriarchal consciousness, our familiar head-ego, often knows nothing of what goes on in the deeper center of consciousness in the heart.

For it is essential to bear in mind that the processes of matriarchal consciousness have their relation to an ego and can therefore not be described as unconscious. To be sure, this ego is of a different kind than the one familiar to us in patriarchal consciousness, but it nevertheless plays an active part in the processes of matriarchal consciousness. Its presence constitutes the difference between human functioning at the matriarchal stage and a totally unconscious existence.

The common identification of our ego with patriarchal head-consciousness and the corresponding unrelatedness to matriarchal consciousness often leads to our not knowing what is really happening to us. In such cases we find out later that we have been deeply impressed by things, situations, and people, of which our head-ego has taken no cognizance whatever. Then, the other way round, a seemingly dull lack of reaction may appear in someone—often a woman—whose head cannot react promptly, but whose heart-consciousness has "conceived." The fact that, like lightning, something has "struck" and been realized will become visible later in the fruitfulness of a personality change. Here the saying of Heraclitus holds true: "Nature loves to hide itself."[11]

The moment of conception is veiled and mysterious, often submitted to by the ego of matriarchal consciousness without any awareness on the part of the head-ego. But a deeper introspection, taking dreams, images, and fantasies into account, will show that in the matriarchal consciousness the moment and the event have been registered, and have by no means passed without a consciousness participating.

There is much meaning in the veiling of these moments of conception that are often so vitally important. Growth needs stillness and invisibility, not loudness and light. It is no accident that the symbols of patriarchal consciousness are daylight and the sun. The validity of this law, for biological as for psychological increase, is confirmed by Nietzsche, that great connoisseur of the creative soul, when he says: "In the state of pregnancy we hide ourselves."[12]

It is not under the burning rays of the sun but in the cool reflected light of the moon, when the darkness of unconsciousness is at the full, that the creative process fulfills itself; the night, not the day, is the time of procreation. It wants darkness and quiet, secrecy, muteness, and hiddenness. Therefore, the moon is lord of life and growth in opposition to the lethal, devouring sun. The moist night time is the time of sleep, but also of healing and recovery. For this reason, the moon-god, Sin, is a physician, and it is said in a cuneiform inscription of his healing plant that "after the sun goes down and with a veiled head, it [the plant] must

11. Diels, *Heraklit,* Fragment 123.

12. Friedrich Nietzsche, *Gesammelte Werke,* vol. 11 (Munich: Musarion Verlag, 1924), 58.

be encircled with a magic ring of flour, and cut before the sun rises."[13] Here we see, associated with the magic circle and with flour, the mystery symbol of "veiling" that belongs to the moon and the secretness of the night. The realms of healing and healer, healing plant and recuperative growth, meet in this configuration.[14] It is the regenerating power of the unconscious that in nocturnal darkness or by the light of the moon performs its task, a *mysterium in a mysterium*, working from out of itself, out of nature, with no aid from the head-ego. This is why healing pills and herbs are ascribed to the moon, and their secrets guarded by women, or better by womanliness, which belongs to the moon.

Here the symbolism of vegetative growth is to be interpreted in the wide sense that conceives every symbol to be a synthesis of inner as well as outer reality. To the nocturnal realm of the healing moon belong the regenerating power of sleep that heals the body and its wounds, the darkness where the recovery takes place, and also those events in the soul that in obscurity, by processes only the heart can know, allow men to "outgrow" their insolvable crises.

It is not, as has been thought, because the moon often looks green in the east, that green has been supposed to be the color of the moon;[15] it is because of the moon's inherent kinship with vegetation, of which it is said: "When Sin's word descends to the earth, the green comes forth."[16] This green of Osiris, of Chidher, of Shiva's sprout, and of the green alchemical stone, is not only the color of physical development but also of the development of the spirit and the soul. The moon as ruler of matriarchal consciousness is connected with a specific knowledge and a particular form of comprehension. This is consciousness that has come to birth, spirit as something born, light as the offspring of night.

Comprehension, as fruit, belongs to the essence of matriarchal consciousness. As Nietzsche put it: "Everything about woman is a riddle,

---

13. Alfred Jeremias, *Handbuch der altorientalischen Geisteskultur* (Berlin/Leipzig: Walter de Gruyter & Co., 1929), 240.

14. Karl Kerényi, *Asklepios: Archetypal Image of the Physician's Existence*, translated by Ralph Manheim (New York: Pantheon Books, 1959); and C.A. Meier, *Ancient Incubation and Modern Psychotherapy*, translated by Monica Curtis (Evanston, Ill.: Northwestern University Press, 1967 [1949]).

15. The symbol of silver that belongs to the moon and, among other things connected with it, the "silver age" of Hesiod, will not be included in this discussion.

16. Jeremias, *Handbuch*, 248.

and everything about woman has one solution. It is called pregnancy."
Again and again the Tree of Life is a moon-tree and its fruit the delicious
fruit of the full moon. The draft, or "pill of immortality," sublime knowledge, illumination, ecstasy, all these are the radiant fruit of the tree of
transforming growth. Also, in India, the moon is King Soma, the intoxicating juice, of which it is said: "As King Soma, the self of nourishment,
I worship him."[17]

We have seen that the moon is lord of fertility and of fertility magic.
This magic associated with matriarchal consciousness is always used for
the increase or insurance of growth, in contrast to the directed magic
of the will, the magic act that, like a hunting spell, for instance, is a tool
of active, male, patriarchal consciousness. Processes of growth are processes of transformation and subject to the self. Matriarchal consciousness mirrors these processes and in its specific way accompanies and
supports them. On the other hand, form-giving processes, in which the
initiative and activity lie with the ego, belong to the domain of the masculine, patriarchal spirit.

To "carry a knowledge and allow it to ripen means, at the same time,
to "accept" it; and acceptance, which here includes the idea of "assimi-
lation," is a typically feminine form of activity, not to be confused with
passive submission or drifting. The comparative passivity of matriarchal consciousness is not due to any incapacity for action, but rather
to an awareness of subjection to a process in which it can "do" nothing,
but can only "let happen." In all decisive life situations, the feminine, in
a far greater degree than the nothing-but masculine, is subjected to the
numinous elements in nature or, still better, has these "brought home"
to it. Therefore, its relation to nature and to God is more familiar and
intimate, and its tie to an anonymous transpersonal allegiance forms
earlier and goes deeper than its personal tie to a man.

Although matriarchal consciousness exists in all human beings and
plays an important role in men, especially if they are creative, women
are still the real representatives of this consciousness, even now when
they have a patriarchal consciousness at their disposal too, and the
opposition between the two attitudes has become a source of deep conflict. For woman has held the attitude of receptivity and acceptance,

17. Paul Deussen, *Sechzig Upanishaden* (Leipzig: F.A. Brockhaus, 1897), 53.

which is basic to matriarchal consciousness, since the beginning of time. She takes this attitude for granted. It is not only during the menstrual period that, to live wisely, she must place her harmony with the moon above the desires and plans of the masculine side of her ego-consciousness. Pregnancy and birth bring total psycho-biological changes also, demanding and presupposing adaptations and adjustments lasting for years on end. In regard to the unknown nature of the child, its character, its sex—a matter of decisive importance in many cultures, both matriarchal and patriarchal—its health, its fate, in all these things, woman is delivered over to the mercy and power of God, and condemned, as an ego, to helpless non-activity and non-intervention. Similarly, at a later stage, she is subjected in an entirely different way from men to the overwhelming force of a love-relation. For this reason, the male faith in the ego and in consciousness is alien to women; indeed, it seems to them slightly absurd and childish. From this stems the profound skepticism and the kind of indifference with which they tend to react toward patriarchal consciousness and the masculine mental world, especially when, as frequently happens, they confuse the two worlds of spirit and conscious-ness. Masculinity is attached to the ego and to consciousness; it has deliberately broken the relation to nature and to destiny in which matriarchal consciousness is so deeply rooted. The patriarchal emphasis on the ego, on will and freedom, contradicts the feminine experience of the "potencies and powers" of the unconscious and of fate, of the way that existence depends on the non-ego and the "thou."

The subdued activity of the ego at the matriarchal stage accords with its preference—as contrasted to that of the head-ego—for the attitude of an observing consciousness. It is more concerned with awareness and attentiveness than with directed thought or judgment. Observant matriarchal consciousness must not be confused with the sensation function of masculine ego-consciousness, or with its aloofness, which leads to scientific objectivity. Matriarchal consciousness is directed by attendant feelings and intuitions that are based on half-conscious processes and assist the emotionally participating ego in its task of orientation.

Matriarchal consciousness reflects unconscious processes, sums them up, and guides itself by them; that is, it behaves more or less passively, without willed ego-intentions. It functions as a kind of total realization in which the whole psyche participates, and in which the ego has the task of turning the libido toward a particular psychic event and intensifying its effect, rather than using the experience as a basis for abstract conclusions and an expansion of consciousness. The typical activity of this observing consciousness is contemplation. In contemplation, the energies are directed toward an emotionally colored content, event, or center, with which the ego establishes a relation and by which it allows itself to be filled and permeated; from this it never withdraws or abstracts, as in an extremely patriarchal consciousness.

The observant, emotionally determined nature of the moon-spirit is designated in the German language by words belonging to the root Sinn, signifying: to muse, to have in mind, to ponder, to consider and to be contemplative; also contemplation, bent of mind, as well as senses and sensual, and last, not least, the *Eigensinn* (self-will, stubbornness), which the male usually ascribes to the female. Matriarchal consciousness circumambulates and broods; it lacks the purposiveness of directed thought, of logical conclusion and judgment. Its characteristic action is a movement around a circle, a contemplation (*Betrachtung,* once interpreted by Jung as *trächtigmachen,* making pregnant). It has not the direct aim of masculine consciousness, nor the knife-sharp edge of its analysis. Matriarchal consciousness is more interested in the meaningful than in facts and dates, and is oriented teleologically to organic growth rather than to mechanical or logical causation.

Since the process of cognition in such a "moon-consciousness" is a pregnancy and its product a birth, a process in which the whole personality participates, its "knowledge" cannot be imparted, accounted for, or proved. It is an inner possession, realized and assimilated by the personality but not easily discussed, for the inner experience behind it is scarcely capable of adequate verbal expression and can hardly be transmitted to anyone who has not undergone the same experience.

For this reason, a plain and simple masculine consciousness finds the "knowledge" of matriarchal consciousness unverifiable, willful, and, par excellence, mystic. This, in fact, is in a positive sense the heart of the matter. It is the same kind of knowledge that is revealed in the true mysteries and in mysticism; it consists not of imparted truths but of experienced transformations, and so necessarily has validity only for people who have passed through a similar experience. For them, Goethe's advice still holds:

Sagt es niemand, nur den Weisen,
Weil die Menge gleich verhöhnet.

Tell it to none, but to the wise
For the crowd is quick in scoffing.[18]

This is to say that the realizations of matriarchal consciousness are conditioned by the personality that has them. They are not abstract and de-emotionalized, for matriarchal consciousness conserves the tie with the unconscious realms from which its knowledge springs. Its insights are therefore often in direct opposition to those of masculine consciousness, which ideally consist of isolated and abstract conscious con-tents, free of emotionalism and possessing a universal validity unaffected by personal factors.

A fundamental trend of Western development has been to expand the domain of patriarchal consciousness and draw to it everything that could possibly be added. Yet matriarchal consciousness is by no means an outdated mode of functioning or an area of undeveloped contents that only lethargy has kept from evolving to the patriarchal level. What the moon-side perceives is in large part, at least to the contemporary psyche, beyond the grasp of scientific understanding. It relates to those general experiences of life that have always been the subject matter of mysteries and religions, and belong to the domain of wisdom, not to that of science.

The moon-spirit bestows culture too, but not in the sense that stargazing and astrology have led to mathematics and astronomy; rather, the celestial prototype of its cultural influence is the "fruit that begets itself," the conqueror of death and bestower of rebirth. As lord of ghosts and the departed, it summons the natural and spiritual powers of the unconscious to arise from the watery depths, when their time is come, and so bestows upon mankind not only growth and sustenance, but also prophecy, poetry, wisdom, and immortality.

Matriarchal consciousness experiences the dark and mysterious process of growing comprehension as something in which the self functions as a totality. The self here dominates as the (male) moon, but above and beyond its moon-aspect, it rules as the Great Mother, as the whole-

---

18. "Selige Sehnsucht," in Johann Wolfgang von Goethe, *West-östlicher Divan* (Stuttgart: J.G. Cotta'sche Buchhandlung, 1820), 30.

ness of the nocturnal. Because of its relation to growth, matriarchal consciousness presupposes this unbroken connection with the root-bed of all growing things, with the nocturnal mother—a connection broken on principle and with heroic determination by the masculine ego; yet for matriarchal consciousness, the influence of the Great Mother and that of the masculine moon often seem to come together in the moon symbol. The relationship, amounting to "participation" between the matriarchal ego and the moon, like that of the Great Mother herself, goes further than partnership with a moon-lover, it reaches identity.

Not only is the likeness to the hermaphroditic nature of the Great Mother shown by the reception of the moon-spirit, the lord and lover from without, as may be supposed at once rightly and wrongly, but also by the carrying within itself of its own masculine side, as a divinity, a son-lover, and at once a father and a child.

The ego of matriarchal consciousness experiences the fructifying power of the moon as the fructifying side of the unconscious, as a portion of the power of the uroboric Great Mother.[19] And through this experience of unbroken union with the wholeness appearing before it in the Great Mother image, it can see its own likeness. The wholeness of the Great Mother, like its own, encircles what it conceives, and recognizes the engenderer as something born of itself, as the son and fruit of its own growth.

So the moon has not only a male manifestation as the center of the spiritual world of matriarchal consciousness; it has also a feminine manifestation as the highest form of the feminine spirit-self, as Sophia, as wisdom. It is a wisdom relating to the indissoluble and paradoxical unity of life and death, of nature and spirit, to the laws of time and fate, of growth, of death and death's overcoming. This figure of feminine wisdom accords with no abstract, unrelated code of law by which dead stars or atoms circulate in empty space; it is a wisdom that is bound and stays bound to the earth, to organic growth, and to ancestral experience. It is the wisdom of the unconscious, of the instincts, of life, and of relationship.

---

19. The uroboros, because of its essential duality includes, among other things, male and female, maternal and paternal. While the female-maternal uroboros rules over the psychological phase of matriarchy, the male uroboros, in which the actively procreative and mobile side of the uroboros is manifested, leads over into patriarchy.

Hence, matriarchal consciousness is the wisdom of the earth, of peasants and, naturally, of women. The teachings of China, particularly of the *I Ching* and of Lao tzu, are an expression of this matriarchal consciousness, which loves the hidden and the dark, and has time. It renounces quick results, prompt reactions, and visible effects. More turned to the night than to the day, it dreams and watches more than it wakes and acts. It has less love for brightness and clarity than seems desirable to patriarchal consciousness, which, turning its back to the moon-side, only too gladly ignores its own dependence upon the dark aspect of the unconscious. Matriarchal wisdom is paradoxical. It never separates and juxtaposes opposites with the clear discrimination of patriarchal consciousness; rather, it relates them to one another by an "as well as" or an "also."

From this point of view—not to be misinterpreted—matriarchal consciousness is relativistic, for it is less oriented to the absolute unambiguity of truth than to a wisdom that remains imbedded in a cosmopsychological system of ever-changing forces. This relativistic attitude often may even appear like enmity toward the "absolute," if a difference in kind and a tendency toward relationship can be termed enmity.

The dependence of matriarchal consciousness upon its partner, the moon-spirit, its consonance with the moon-spirit's changing phases, contains an element of Eros, a dependence on the "thou" of the partner as moon-lover, which distinguishes matriarchal from patriarchal consciousness as a consciousness of relationship. Patriarchal consciousness is free to act and think when, how, and what it wants. In its detached, abstract way, it is self-sufficient or ego-sufficient, supreme within the circle of its conscious contents. But matriarchal consciousness is not self-sufficient; it is bound to the moon and to the unconscious and, aware of its dependence, adjusts itself accordingly.

For this reason the wisdom of the moon-Sophia lacks that abstract, non-individual, universal, and absolute character that the patriarchal male asserts to be the highest spirituality, revering it as the celestial spirit-sphere of sun and daylight, and setting it above the moon-world. From this point of view, the moon-spirit of matriarchal consciousness is "only" moon-spirit, "only" soul, and the eternal feminine. But by forfeiting the character of "remote" divinity, matriarchal consciousness retains the milder and less blinding light of the human spirit. Woman's wisdom is non-speculative; it is close to nature and life, bound to fate and to living reality. Its illusionless view of actuality may shock an idealistic, masculine mentality; yet it is related to this actuality as nourisher, helper, comforter, and lover, and leads it beyond death to ever renewed transformation and rebirth.

The moon-wisdom of waiting, accepting, ripening, admits everything into its totality and transforms it and, along with it, its own being. It is always concerned with wholeness, with shaping and realizing, with the creative. One must never forget that the creative is by its inherent nature related to matriarchal consciousness. It is not the conscious but the unconscious that is creative, and every creative achievement, like a pregnancy, presupposes an attitude of patience and relatedness such as we have found characteristic of matriarchal consciousness.

However, while all creative cultural achievement—at least in its highest form—represents a synthesis of receptive matriarchal and formative patriarchal consciousness, woman's predominant dependence upon matriarchal consciousness and its form of wisdom entails, with all its blessings, some inherent dangers. It is certainly consonant with the moon-spirit and the process of growth that silence and realization should come before formulation and understanding; but woman's tendency to realization, one of the creative elements of matriarchal consciousness, often gets entangled in mere naturalness.

In that early phase of its development, the "self-establishment" phase,[20] when the feminine can without danger still remain caught in the Great Mother, matriarchal consciousness is quite unaware of being dominated by the unconscious. But even when the matriarchal ego becomes conscious of its separate existence, it still adheres to the basic condition of its former existence, which is never to be split. Even when the feminine, as will be shown, has to progress from the task of self-establishment to that of self-surrender, it still wants to be totally involved. It is never satisfied with the fulfillment of a partial psychic structure such as a conscious differentiation of the ego; the feminine wishes the whole of itself included. That, on the spiritual or psychological plane, means realization.

But here woman's nature often plays a trick. Instead of realizing, she concretizes, and, by a natural projection, transposes the creative pro-

---

20. See Part I of this paper in *Eranos Yearbook* 18.

cess of pregnancy onto the external plane. That is to say, woman takes the symbols of this phase of matriarchal consciousness literally; she loves, becomes pregnant, bears, nourishes, cherishes, and so on, and lives her femininity outwardly but not in the inner world. This tendency may explain the smallness of her spiritual achievements as compared to men, her lack of creative productivity. It seems to a woman (rightly or wrongly?) that to be the source of life in pregnancy and birth is creative enough. Matriarchal consciousness is written into a woman's body, and through her body she lives in outer actuality all which for a man must become a psychological happening, if it is to be realized.[21] In this sense, man, with his developed patriarchal consciousness, is a step ahead, since nature permits him to experience the matriarchal phase of consciousness only as a spiritual advancement, and not in concrete form.

As a result, when mankind is forced to come to patriarchal consciousness and to break with the unconscious, matriarchal consciousness, like matriarchy, and along with it, the moon, becomes something negative to be surmounted. Any development, at any stage, that strives toward patriarchal consciousness, toward the sun, looks on the moon-spirit as the spirit of regression, as the terrible mother, as a witch. Whether this negative moon is experienced as masculine or feminine, it is in either case a symbol of the devouring unconscious. Especially as the dark moon, it becomes the blood-sucker, the child-murderer, the eater of human flesh;[22] it symbolizes the danger of inundation by the unconscious, of moodiness, lunacy, and madness. The English "to moon," to be melancholy, to waste time, shows that to be "withdrawn" can mean to be "drawn to the moon" with its dangerous pull toward the unconscious.

Here, as everywhere, comes the question as to what value a psychic phase has at any special stage of development. Moon-consciousness or matriarchal consciousness is creative and productive at the beginning and end. Moon-light is the first light to illumine the dark world of the

21. Not entirely without justification, and certainly not without humor, one woman's psycho-analytic theory—a kind of answer to the penis-envy imputed to the feminine by man—was that the cultural achievement of man is only a compensation for his incapacity to really give birth, and so stems, in a way, from his "uterus-envy."

22. Robert Briffault, *The Mothers: A Study of the Origins of Sentiments and Institutions*, 3 vols. (New York: Macmillan, 1927).

unconscious, whence consciousness is born and to which it remains bound; and all things that are child-like, growing, creative, and feminine remain faithful to their relation to the moon-spirit.

But as development goes on, that which was a progression out from the unconscious comes to be a holding fast to the unconsciousness. At this point, the new and superior sun world comes into opposition with the world of the moon, as patriarchy does with matriarchy, when they are considered as two psychological phases. Only in later periods of development, when patriarchy has fulfilled itself or gone to absurd lengths, losing its connection with Mother Earth, does individuation bring about a reversal. Then, patriarchal sun-consciousness reunites with the earlier, more fundamental phase, and matriarchal consciousness, with its central symbol, the moon, arises from the deep, imbued with the regenerating power of its primal waters, to celebrate the ancient *hieros gamos* of moon and sun on a new and higher plane, the plane of the human psyche.

For the masculine as for the feminine, wholeness is attainable only when in a union of opposites, the day and the night, the upper and the lower, the patriarchal consciousness and the matriarchal, come to their own kind of productivity and mutually supplement and fructify one another.

The Jewish Midrash relates that at the beginning of creation the sun and moon were of equal size, but the moon, because it committed a sin, was made smaller, and the sun became the ruling star of the universe. However, God's promise to the moon foretells the re-establishment of the original situation:

> At that time thou wilt again be large as the sun;
> And the moon's light will be like the sun's light.[23]

23. Micha Josef bin Gorion, *Die Sagen der Juden*, vol. 1: *Von der Urzeit* (Frankfurt a. M.: Rütten & Loening, 1913), 16.

The Devouring Father

MURRAY STEIN

The devouring mother has become a well-known archetypal reality in the world of depth psychology. Jung describes the mother-devoured personality in its neurotic form (*CW*9.2, §§20-22); its most extreme forms appear as the endogenous psychoses, schizophrenia and manic-depression. Not quite so familiar is the archetype of the devouring father. Here one could speak of the most extreme form as social psychosis.

If at the one pole the archetypal father is guardian of his children and mighty fortress against the threats of the outer world, at the other he is devourer through his rigid insistence on conventional thought, feeling, and behavior. The phenomenological reflection of this negative side of the father archetype is consciousness tied, bound, swallowed in convention and habit, in attention to duty as defined by prevailing collective norms. A gastric flood—of values, thought patterns, tastes, dispositions, attitudes, opinions—from the prevailing culture digest away all traces of individual experience and spontaneous reaction.

Leo Tolstoy's story "The Death of Ivan Ilyich" draws a masterful portrait of father-devoured consciousness. Tolstoy introduces Ivan as:

> the son of an official whose career in Petersburg in various ministries and departments had been such as leads men to positions from which, by reason of their long service and the official rank they have attained, they cannot be discharged, although it is obvious that they are unfit to perform any useful duty, and for whom, therefore, posts are specially created, which though fictitious carry

salaries of from six to ten thousand roubles that are not fictitious
and on which they go on living to an advanced age.[1]

No mention is made in the story of Ivan's mother. His father is clearly a
representation of the senex in his form of the old king who should die
but stubbornly goes on ruling.

Two details underscore Ivan's connection to his father. The first is a
sum of money that his father gives him after he has earned his university
degree in law. With this money he buys his outfit: he orders clothes from
"Scharmer's" and adds to his wardrobe other "new fashionable belong-
ings—a trunk, linen, uniform, shaving and toilet requisites and a travel-
ing rug—all ordered and purchased at the very best shops." These things
in hand, Ivan sets off for the provinces "to take up the post of confiden-
tial clerk and emissary to the governor which had been obtained for
him by his father."[2] Standing thus conspicuously in the background, the
father opens the jaws for Ivan's entry into the structures of established
power.

Ivan, too, like his father, enters government service. His profession
is law. The world of law courts is the world of the father, in his role as
restrictor and overseer. The courts adjudicate grievances in a more or
less orderly way, provide channels for prosecution and appeal, interpret the laws of the land. As the final authority on questions of right and
wrong, allowed and prohibited, they reinforce the collective values of
society. In short, they maintain and support the interlocking attitudes
and values that form the backbone of a culture.

In Ivan's character we find a highly differentiated study of the father-
devoured personality. The author comments:

> As a student he was already just what he was to remain for the
> rest of his life: a capable, cheerful, good-natured and sociable fel-
> low, though strict in the performance of what he considered his
> duty; and he considered as his duty whatever was so considered
> by those in authority over him.[3]

Especially noteworthy in this passage is the stability and intransigence
of Ivan's attitude: what he was as a student he was to remain for the rest

1. Leo Tolstoy, *The Cossacks/The Death of Ivan Ilyich/Happy Ever After*, translated by
Rosemary Edmonds (Baltimore: Penguin Books, 1960), 110.
2. Ibid., 111.
3. Ibid., 110.

of his life. As we shall see later, this sort of permanence is a primary goal of the archetypal devouring father. A second point to note is what happens to Ivan's conscience:

> As a law student he had done things which had before that seemed to him vile and at the same time had made him feel disgusted with himself; but later on when he saw that such conduct was practised by people of high standing and not considered wrong by them, he came not exactly to regard those actions of his as all right but simply to forget them entirely or not be at all troubled by their recollection.[4]

The reactions of individual conscience are superceded by the authorities "out there," by the tastes, values, proclivities of those who represent the currently dominant forces of collective consciousness. At adaptation to so-called outer reality, Ivan is a genius.

Tolstoy brings this development of the collectivization of Ivan's consciousness to an exquisite climax when he has him furnish his new apartment. Choosing each item with anxious care, tossing in his bed as he agonizes over this divan or that, losing interest in the proceedings at court as his mind wanders to the subject of draperies, carpets, and picture frames, Ivan exercises the determined discrimination of the possessed. The result is, in Ivan's mind, both charming and ideal. In reality, however,

> it was just what is commonly seen in the houses of people who are not exactly wealthy but who want to look like wealthy people, and so succeed only in looking like all the others of their own kind.[5]

What is meant to express most precisely his individuality brings forth only the most collective in him.

Significantly, Ivan's relationship to his wife deteriorates as his worldly fortunes grow, as he becomes more and more absorbed in the life of the law courts and whirl of social competition. Finally he seals off this problematic area in his life with a "rational" policy:

> He required of it [i.e., marriage] only those conveniences—a wife to manage his house, meals and a bed—which it could give him and, in particular, the keeping up of appearances as ordained by

---

4. Ibid., 111.
5. Ibid., 121.

public opinion. For the rest he looked for cheerful amiability and if he found it was very grateful; but if he encountered antagonism and peevishness he promptly retreated into his other world of official duties, and there found satisfaction.[6]

As Ivan retreats from the feminine world of wife, daughter and family, his life becomes progressively more uncreative and soulless. We watch how he stifles all unconscious promptings toward an individual attitude, how he boxes in and suffocates his unorthodox and unconventional "children," how he imposes abstractions and rules on the arbitrary urgings of Eros. Ivan is a man of many acquaintances and no friends. Orderliness, punctuality and habit tyrannize him. In court and out his attitude is severely professional:

> He got up at nine, drank his coffee, read the newspaper, then donned his undress uniform and went to the Law Courts. Then he fell instantly into his well-worn harness and prepared to deal with petitions, inquiries in the office, the office itself, and the sessions—public and administrative. In all this the thing was to exclude everything with the sap of life in it, which always disturbs the regular round of official business, and not to admit any sort of relations with people except official relations, and then only on official grounds.[7]

In his mid-forties, at the height of success in his professional life, Ivan is struck by a mysterious, undiagnosable disease. As his illness draws to an end, pulling death slowly over him like a shroud, he realizes a truth about his life:

> It struck him that those scarcely detected inclinations of his to fight against what the most highly placed people regarded as good, those scarcely noticeable impulses which he had immediately suppressed, might have been the real thing and all the rest false. And his professional duties, and his family, and all his social and official interests might all have been false.[8]

Those "scarcely detected inclinations" and "scarcely noticeable impulses," which got more and more heavily layered over by the hardening sedi-

---

6. Ibid., 116.
7. Ibid., 123.
8. Ibid., 157.

ments of his one-sided attitude, are the half-articulate voices of child-hood, the stirrings of creative (and destructive) impulses, the inher-ent inclination to develop an individual point of view. They refer to the voices of the unconscious, that eternal mother of renewed forms of life, "the mysterious root of all growth and change" (Jung, *CW* 9.1, §72). They are the devoured children.

One must add that equally swallowed by the father is Ivan's polar opposite—i.e., the obsessive anti-authoritarian, the deliberate eccentric, the systematic non-conformist—devoured not by identification with col-lective consciousness, but by his severe allergy against it. This counter-type finds it equally impossible to experience life individually. His neg-ative father complex has him in maw.

Greek mythology, in the figures of Ouranos, Kronos. and Zeus, offers a differentiated picture of the archetypal background of father-devoured consciousness. All three are gods, but not merely ordinary gods: they are dominant gods, kings, undisputed rulers. All three, too, are not only fathers, but devouring fathers.

Each of these three instances of the devouring father presents a dif-ferent nuance in the archetypal pattern. Ouranos is perhaps the most malicious, certainly the most archaic and ferocious of the three. He does not, however, devour his children directly, but pushes them back into their mother, Gaia, materia, and imprisons them there. Ouranos, the sky, defends his position by keeping his young unconscious, mother-bound, encapsulated in dull day-in, day-out *materia*. One sees in this arche-typal configuration an enormous split between spirit and *materia,* sym-bolic understanding and concrete literalism, mother and father. So out of reach and beyond question is the spirit of the times that all creativity and innovation remain locked in the sphere of practical tinkering with the material environment.

Consciousness dominated by Ouranos results in conventionality through gross unconsciousness: "this is the way it's always been done"; "this is what I was taught as a child." The subject is unconscious of his attitudes and presuppositions and displays a nearly total lack of self-awareness and poverty of insight into his psychic background. Con-vention, tradition, collective values are unconsciously assimilated, and the new, the child, the creative future development, remains locked in the mother.

In this archetypal pattern, consciousness is exceedingly primitive; individual consciousness is practically non-existent, group consciousness overwhelmingly in the ascendancy. Jung, following Lévy-Bruhl, names this state of affairs *participation mystique* with the group.

Ouranos is also an author of psychosomatic symptoms: the repressed children *materialize*, and the somatic base (Gaia) groans with the burden. Tumors, gastric disorders, various hysterical symptoms appear mysteriously, and suffering comes physically, materially; the body suffers, the mind fails to understand, and the drama plays itself out in the darkness of physis. Primitive peoples know how to treat such disorders: the shaman, or priest, or witch-doctor confronts the spirits of the disease; he flies to "the other side" and discovers them there. His is a method of dredging the "children" out of *materia* and treating them for what they are, i.e., spirits.

In the bloody victory of Kronos over his sky-father, and the subsequent emergence of a new order, we must note a central motif in the mythologem of the devouring father: change comes through the revolutionary act of the son. Puer leaps high and tears down senex. One of Ouranos's sons finds release and brutally castrates the father.

Freud placed the fear of castration in the son. Our myth would place it more properly on the side of the father: not son but father is the victim of castration. If the threat to the son (Kronos) is repression and imprisonment, the threat to the father is castration.

Castration is the ultimate act of unmanning and humiliation. It is also deprivation of the masculine ability to fertilize and impregnate; it is sterilization of the spirit. But in our myth its meaning reaches still further: it is the heroic act that separates heaven and earth and thereby releases the children of heaven from their prison in earth. It signifies therefore the process of spiritualization, of making psyche. Contents that were formerly locked in *materia* now become the Titanic personalities. This tendency to spiritualize will also, as we shall see later, characterize Kronos's acts of child-devouring. acts of child-devouring Kronos, whose name means "time," brings in an essential aspect of ego-consciousness. Unlike Ouranos, who is the eternal, infinite sky, Kronos underlies our perception of past-present-future, our orientation in time. His castration of Ouranos, therefore, means the end of eternal blind reproduction, of purely instinctual fecundity, age following age endlessly, driven on by unself-conscious spirit. After the castration of Ouranos this kind of creativity is no longer possible. Genius enters the stage of time—and self-consciousness. The castrating instrument of Kronos becomes the scythe of Father Time.

If Kronos is at first puer and carrier of new spirit, he quickly himself turns to devouring father. From his parents he learns that one of his children is destined to overcome him. At this he digs in his heels and through the stratagem of eating his children tries to resist the law of life that sons bury their fathers. The mythologem of the devouring father rests on a principle of eternal revolution, son replacing father, puer overthrowing senex, new destroying old. It is a myth of changes. Kronos, as the puer who comes to power, knows the treachery and energy of the young and is determined to resist their dynamic advance.

Whereas the strategy of Ouranos is to keep his potential rivals, his children, unconscious through repression in *materia,* the strategy of Kronos is to incorporate them and thus to spiritualize or psychologize them, thereby severing them from their instinctual origins. Through this process of spiritualization the children are deprived of their radical transformative power.

In culture, the prevailing dominants of collective life might say: "Provide a narrow path by which the youngster can advance in society and secure a niche in the established order; make sure the alternative is complete failure and annihilation." One finds this state of affairs at its most extreme in certain periods of Chinese history, where the only road to social acceptance and advancement lay in rigid adherence to a labyrinthine system of codes and custom. In its milder forms this attitude of culture may even sound generous: society shows willingness to incorporate youth into its established structures. But its strategy is effectively lethal, for it seeks to make of its citizens men who are totally dominated by culture and the social milieu and cut off from the creative (and destructive) forces of the unconscious. Ivan Ilyich illustrates this disaster. So do the "good Christians" who have no shadow and who twist all unconscious contents to positive, spiritual ends. By this strategy the dominants of collective consciousness maintain their position and preserve their power, but simultaneously devour the true child, the possibility of a future development along new lines.

Under Kronos, consciousness is finely tuned to the prevailing values and attitudes of an outer collective, be it secular society at large, a church group, a political party, or whatnot. It is threatened by stirrings in the unconscious, by "infantile" impulses, "crazy" thoughts, "childish" reactions. It either rejects these unwanted children out of hand or more often tries to find in them a positive spiritual content, "child*like*" reactions, "interesting" ideas, "creative" movements of the soul. This act of splitting positive and negative, spiritual and instinctual, creative and destructive is Kronos swallowing his children. For the future most often lies with the dark children, who naturally pose a threat to the established order of things: "a man's destiny is always shaped at the point where his fear lies."[9]

Kronos-determined consciousness seeks to twist all interests, passions, and spontaneous ideas to the service of its own conscious goals. What one swallows is meant to nourish and promote one's own life; the digestive process rejects the "trash" and absorbs the nourishment. So one plays hard in order to work better, invents to sell, creates to reap the rewards of personal fame and prestige, naturally all the while denying the shadowy aspect of the power motive. Everything goes to build the ego; the children of the unconscious are meant to support, Atlas-like, an edgy and insecure ego.

In all its forms the devouring father archetype presses consciousness toward conventionality. Under Kronos, consciousness is swallowed up by the spirit of the age and loses contact with instinctual life, the earth, Rhea. This radical split between conscious and unconscious serves the interests of the prevailing dominants of culture by depriving consciousness of instinctual, irrational reactions.

Kronos is secretly allied with earth mother Gaia against his own wife and children: Gaia warns him of the threat from a future son. So, in a sense, the ambition of Kronos is rooted in the mother, or perhaps more precisely in her animus. This alliance is typical of puer psychology and accounts in part for his frequently radical and extremely swift shifts into senex. If on the one side puer carries spirit and brings in the new age, on the other he is allied with materia and is thereby fatally

---

9. Aniela Jaffé, "The Creative Phases in Jung's Life," *Spring: An Annual of Archetypal Psychology and Jungian Thought* (1972): 164.

tempted to concretize his fantasies and to hang on to these concretizations. His heroic fantasy, given concrete expression, turns into spiritual tyranny. Kronos-devoured consciousness is therefore held in place by two forces: on the one side, its conservative senex aspect is deeply rooted in instinct, earth mother; on the other, the forces for change are deprived of this dynamic connection.

But Kronos can be tricked. He is deceived, however, not by one of his clever children, but by Rhea, who in this instance performs the role of the Great Mother in her aspect as protector of children. Rhea deceives Kronos with a blanket-covered stone and delivers the real child, Zeus, to a protected cave in Crete where he is raised by three Dictaean Ash-nymphs.[10] Through the agency of Rhea the dynamic movement toward change through the revolutionary son takes a new leap forward. The cycle is again put into motion, but as Kronos is different in nuance from Ouranos so Zeus is different from Kronos. The development within this archetype is not therefore purely cyclic but more in the nature of a spiral that with each turn acquires new characteristics.

Zeus leads to power the Olympian gods, and the old Titanic pantheon is locked away in Tartarus. But Zeus, too, betrays traces of the devouring father. His first consort is Metis, daughter of the Titans Okeanos and Tethys. Warned by Gaia and Ouranos of the danger posed by a future son of this union, Zeus tricks the pregnant Metis into entering his stomach and keeps her there. He thereby devours his *potential* children. This strategy seems effective, for Zeus maintains his power to the end of the mythological age. He himself bears Metis's child, Athene; in some accounts she springs fully armed from his head. She later becomes his wisest and most trusted counselor.

In contradistinction to Ouranos and Kronos, Zeus bears many children whom he does not devour. Generally he is fond of his children and takes care to look after them. But the myth of Zeus ingesting Metis shows that he, too, like his fathers before him, seeks to stabilize the revolutionary cycle with himself in the dominant position.

Under Zeus, consciousness attains to a much greater degree of flexibility than under Kronos. Looking at the children of Zeus who are

---

10. Karl Kerényi, *The Gods of the Greeks*, translated by Norman Cameron (New York: Grove Press, 1960), 92.

allowed to live, one can see what a really remarkable tolerance for opposites the Olympian world has: Apollo and Dionysos, Athene and Ares, Artemis and Helen. The *Iliad* tells of the deep-going strains on Olympus; Zeus rules but his hand is relatively light. Under Zeus, consciousness is flexible enough to integrate all but the truly revolutionary ideas and forces. One sees emerging the Greek ideal of exercising creativity within a framework of balanced order and harmony. Such impulses and urges as cannot be integrated, the truly revolutionary children, are kept dormant and merely potential in their encapsulated mother; they are kept contained in the belly of Zeus.

If the strategy of Ouranos is locking the children in materia and away from spirit, and that of Kronos is swallowing them in spirit and cutting them off from instinct, the strategy of Zeus is incorporating the anima in spirit and thereby depriving her of fertility, of the capacity for becoming pregnant with revolutionary children. Because he has integrated the anima in this way, Zeus can afford to tolerate his other children.

A capacity for reflection upon and containment of divergent impulses and forces characterize his reign. Athene, the daughter of Metis and Zeus, born through her father's head, embodies this capacity: Athene restrains impulsive aggressiveness, encourages reflection and strategic thinking, and among the heroes favors the wily Odysseus. Athene is her father's daughter, the eternal virgin, the anima of spirit, life turning inward to reflection.[11] Through his relation to Metis-Athene, the senex aspect of Zeus, the devouring father in him is ameliorated and made less extreme. This toning-down of the puer-senex polarity in him accounts for his success where Kronos failed. Under Zeus, consciousness is able to contain and tolerate and let live to a far greater degree than under Kronos where all the children have to be incorporated in spirit. But if the rule of Zeus produces stability, it does so at a certain price: through cancellation of the possibility for revolutionary change, destructive though it may appear at the time, a creative future is also lost. So, in the internal development of this archetype, the more or less tolerant, flexible, reflective senex wins out. This is a gain, and a loss.

---

11. Cf. René Malamud, "The Amazon Problem," *Spring: An Annual of Archetypal Psychology and Jungian Thought* (1971).

The Archetype of Saturn, or
Transformation of the Father

AUGUSTO VITALE

It is often not an easy task to begin to describe a region of the collective unconscious, as I am going to do, because the subject is not a rational one that can be systematically ordered in a logical manner. It is the recollection of many empirical facts that may bring the intuition of an archetypal motif, and so lead to a region of our psyche where each point can be used as the starting point for the description of the region. We can get a sufficient understanding of it only when we have completed our tour.

SOME ASPECTS OF MELANCHOLY

Where can we find the experience of melancholy? I will point out only in short outlines melancholy as found in psychiatry and in some peculiar conditions of so-called normal life, as in mourning, nostalgia, adolescence—also as expressed in special fields of human activity, the arts, philosophical *Weltanschauung* and religion.

After that, we will look for a common motif. This common motif could introduce us, by amplification, into the psychological inquiry of archetypes. We have chosen the archetype of Saturn, of the negative father. Other motifs and archetypal images might prove equally valid, but this question will appear more clearly at the end of the lecture.

The psychical states that we call melancholy all have some characteristics in common. From an objective point of view, there is a lowering of energy level in most of the psychical conscious functions, relationship life and all its expressions are reduced, mental processes and

---

First presented at the C. G. Jung Institute, Summer Semester 1970.

activities are slowed down. Melancholy goes from total inhibition, as in some psychotic depressions, to the lightest gradations of mood, but in all cases there is a subjective consciousness of sorrow bound to a feeling of powerlessness or impotence to will or to use one's own faculties. Let us consider some aspects of melancholy that can be easily observed. At one extreme we encounter the depression of manic-depressive psychosis, which is often simply called "melancholy" or "melancholia." Here is what Jaspers, the philosopher and psychopathologist, says about the characteristic of melancholic depression:

> Its core consists of a deep and unmotivated sadness, in addition to an inhibition of all psychical activities. Besides being felt very painfully by the subject, it is also observable in his objective behavior. All instinctive drives are inhibited; the patient does not desire anything. It ranges from a lessening of the desire for movement and activity to a complete immobility. No decision, no activity can be undertaken by the patient. He lacks psychological associations. Nothing comes to mind; he complains about his deranged memory; he feels his lack of productive capacity and laments his insufficiency, insensibility and emptiness. He experiences this deep affliction as a peculiar sensation in the breast and abdomen, almost as if it could be grasped there. In his deep sadness the world seems to him grey within grey, indifferent and disconsolate. He looks only for the unfavorable and unhappy side of everything. He feels he has had many guilts in the past; the present offers only misfortune and the future looks terrifying with visions of ruin and impoverishment. At this stage of melancholy—anxiety, boredom, and despair show a way out in suicide.[1]

If we take melancholy in its everyday or literary usage, it has the meaning of a gloomy and slack state of mind, a condition of sorrow, of being sunk in meditation and irritability—or, more romantically, a state of vague and resigned dejection, a meditative and intimate pain.

If in the extreme stages inhibition prevails, in all others there are besides the apparent inactivity and apathy an innermost longing, a constant work and torment, a searching without rest, thoughts and fancies that know neither their goals nor their needs. If a desirable goal

---

1. Karl Jaspers, *Psicopatologia Generale* (Rome: Il Pensiero Scientifico, 1964), 115ff.; my translation.

is glimpsed, the subject runs up against a painful inhibition, an unaccountable impotence or an indecisive and inconclusive turning round.

Homesickness without hope, loss of an irreplaceable good, as may be experienced in exile or in the sorrow of mourning; such feelings are contained, so to say, in the state of melancholy and permit the amplification of its meaning.

As in homesickness and mourning, happiness that was known living in that land, or near that precious being, is in the memory boundless. By now everything is dull since such happiness was once known; all existence is conditioned; everyday experiences are continuously measured with this memory, stubbornly compared with it, as if to gain confirmation that what the subject experiences today isn't worth the shadow of that which he has lost.

It is as if there existed some power opposed to the reunion with that which has been lost, an overwhelming, adverse and inflexible power that seems to paralyze the will and provoke that painful feeling of impotence.

All this is quite well illustrated in the melancholy that frequently affects adolescents. The adult world may be perceived by the adolescent as the hard reality, arduous, unpoetic as well as inescapable, in opposition to a sentimentally coloured and cherished world of dreams and poetry generally connected with fabulous memories and the nostalgia of childhood. The melancholy adolescent experiences the irresolution, perplexity and depression of being between two opposite sides of his existence: for him, to grow older is unavoidable, but it means to be deprived of the shining, nostalgic world of childhood. He sees the grown-up world as represented by persons who cannot understand those values and, moreover, who mock them. Contrary to the adolescent, they have power, will and self-assurance, and by their mere existence they emphasize the insufficiency and incompleteness of the young man; they affirm a reality that looks to the adolescent grey and hard.

The melancholy adolescent experiences feelings of inferiority, impotence, guilt, because he doesn't accept the "values" of the grown-up world, and at the same time he experiences bitterness and contempt for a world toward which he nevertheless feels drawn by an invincible underground current. He flees toward what he feels to be a more acceptable atmosphere, the mystic, artistic or philosophical. In his practical life he experiences waste, inconclusiveness, indecisiveness, confusion, as a consequence of contradiction and perplexity, because the attempt to settle the two aspects of life has failed. The melancholy adolescent often indulges in the idea of death as the "desired wreck" that could relieve him from a ruthless reality.

In our experience we encounter other forms of melancholy that help our task of unfolding and amplifying this psychological state and trying to find its unconscious components.

Philosophical pessimism may be considered a systematic display of a temperamental melancholy that is reflected in the thinking and becomes Weltanschauung. It may seem a mere aspect of character, an obsessive tendency to see in life only what is wrong. Every aspect of life brings with it ideas of decadence, disorder, waste, danger, and improvidence, even death and oblivion. In those who experience this pessimism there is the impression that someone must be responsible; as Leopardi, the poet of pessimism, said: "the ugly hidden power which rules for general damage,"[2] or as Hamlet says in his monologue: "the whips and scorns of time" (III, 1, 70).

In these forms of melancholy the world and reality are seen as being endowed with insurmountable power and, on the other hand, an unshakable negativity; man is seen as a toy in the hands of a mocking destiny. Every living thing in which might appear beauty and goodness gives rise at once to the contrary images of death, destruction, corruption. The fragile brings to mind destruction and the ephemeral, illusion and pain.

Until now we have spoken about the negative aspects of melancholy, but there are other manifestations that bring to light the positive side of it, those in which the subject experiences in his memory, imagination or intuition the aspect of existence most longed-for but denied. I refer to that melancholy that may be associated with the experience of the beautiful and the melancholy, perhaps very similar to this, that seizes men in the field of mystical-religious experiences.

On the one hand, the meeting with the fragile flower of beauty provokes once more thoughts linked with the frailty of all things human.

---

2. "A se stesso," *I Canti di Giacomo Leopardi* (Milan: Ulrico Hoepli, 1900), 182–83; my translation.

As Petrarch says: "All things beautiful and mortal pass and do not endure."[3] Or in the words of Heine: "To wither, to be stripped of leaves, even trampled under the rough feet of destiny; such is, my friend, the fate of the beautiful on the earth."[4] Thus, the state of melancholic contemplation is realized in which the most desirable good unites with inevitable condemnation.

But the connection between beauty and melancholy seems to be even deeper and more secret. It is certain that the tie between beauty and melancholy has been experienced by men, perhaps only a certain type of men, for ages. We can quote Socrates in the *Phaedrus*: "when one sees the beauty of here below, remembering the true one, he sprouts wings and burns with the desire to fly; but because he cannot, like a bird he turns his gaze toward the heavens, forgetting things of here below and is accused of being in a state of madness."[5] Or, as Baudelaire says: "Melancholy is the illustrious companion of beauty, to the extent that I cannot conceive any beauty which could not have in itself any unhappiness."[6]

Marsilio Ficino, the fifteenth-century humanist founder of the Platonic Academy in Florence, has given special stress to the close connection between beauty and melancholy. In his *De vita triplici* he puts melancholy as a middle step in a kind of individuation process beginning with the knowing of beauty, which in turn provokes sadness because of its mortality. The members of the Academy say that this state of melancholy is under the sign of Saturn, the planet-god who was also the patron of that Academy. Melancholy and love for beauty provoke the will to generate in order to immortalize life. In other words, melancholy may disclose the way to creative life.

We may, in short, mention the melancholy that may be encountered in religious life. In some persons, the religious experience appears as a sudden crisis. In such cases it is often preceded by a state of melancholy extraordinarily similar to pathological "melancholia":

---

3. *Le Rime di Francesco Petrarca,* edited by Giovanni Mestica (Florence: G. Barbèra, 1896), 345 (son. CCX); my translation.

4. Heinrich Heine, "Deutschland: Ein Wintermärchen," XXIII.93–95; my translation.

5. Plato, *Phaedrus* 249d; my translation.

6. "Journaux intimes," in Charles Baudelaire, *Oeuvres posthumes* (Paris: Société du Mercure de France, 1908), 85; my translation.

...desperation absolute and complete, the whole universe coagulating about the sufferer into a material of overwhelming horror, surrounding him without opening or end. Not the conception or intellectual perception of evil, but the grisly blood-freezing heart-palsying sensation of it close upon one, and no other conception or sensation able to live for a moment in its presence.[7]

The "positive" aspect of the religious experience in such cases is in close relation to the preceding state because the subject has the intuition that he can escape from that unbearable world by a second birth into another world, where prevails the perfect purity of God. Mystics are especially inclined to experience a state of union with the infinite and perfect being, in which all is full of meaning and love—a state that might be considered an opposite pole of melancholy.

ANALOGICAL INVESTIGATION (AMPLIFICATION)

The repetition of certain motifs in a psychological state so frequent and rich in emotion makes us think that we find ourselves in the gravitational field of an archetype. As archetypes are unknowable in themselves, it is useful to look for some manifestations of the same gravitational field in other spheres of human expression.

Mythology generally has a peculiar possibility in research of this type because of the spontaneity, variety and wealth of its expressions. As regards melancholy, a very old tradition, respected even today, associates the name of Saturn with that of melancholy. In Greco-Roman mythology the figures of Saturn and Kronos overlap and therefore we will make reference to both myths. Let us try to analyze the myth of Saturn, keeping in mind the phenomenology of melancholy. Mythical and psychological elements should mutually clarify, amplify and explain each other.

As melancholy is so undifferentiated, elementary and common, it is fitting that it be found in a mythological amplification, equally primeval and archaic. This is the case of the myth of Kronos-Saturn, which tells of the very first origins of human cosmogony; it deals neither with the stage of heroes nor with that of anthropomorphic gods, but with the Titans and the origin of the divine race itself.

---

7. William James, *The Variety of Religious Experience: A Study in Human Nature* (London: Longmans, Green and Co., 1919), 162.

According to Hesiod,[8] the story of Kronos unfolds itself in three stages. At the beginning he is "Kronos the cunning" whose power consists in astuteness and surprise attack, the youngest of the sons of Uranus and Rhea, the original couple. Uranus prevents the birth of his sons out of their mother's body. The mother gives Kronos the sickle with which the son castrates and kills his father, thus freeing himself and the other Titans from the mother's body. In the second stage, Kronos himself becomes king of the gods; but, forewarned by his mother's prophecy, he fears being in turn dethroned by one of his sons, and therefore to avoid this danger he swallows each son his wife Rhea generates.

In a third stage, by means of Rhea's stratagem, the sons are liberated from their father's stomach. Rhea gives her husband a stone in place of the last-born, Jove. The latter, grown up in secret on the island of Crete and protected by the Corybantes, who hide his crying with the noise of their instruments, dethrones Kronos, liberates his brothers and becomes king of the gods. The old god, dethroned, whose symbol remains that of the sickle, is sent to the end of the world, where he will reign over the island of the blessed, god and king of the happy Golden Age.

The story of Saturn[9] coincides with that of Kronos. He is the antique Italic god of agriculture whose symbol is the sickle. Dispossessed by Jove, he finds shelter in the region of Latium where he later becomes king, during a prosperous and ancient age of happy and peaceful life. The feast of Saturn, among the most important of the year, was celebrated in the winter solstice. It was characterized by the exchange of gifts, merry-making, and a temporary abolition of the differences between slave and master. Kronos-Saturn is therefore god of agriculture, of the moon harvest, and also of sowing.

As we attempt to approach the myth beyond the apparent, superficial meaning we begin to perceive the vastness of the horizon and of the forces that come into play. Let us try to grasp intuitively the meaning contained in the myth.

The destiny of Kronos develops in three stages, during which his potentiality unfolds and manifests itself. In the first stage, the birth of Kronos is a violent and revolutionary crisis. Kronos succeeds in coming into the world only at the price of a violent rebellion against his father.

---

8. Hesiod, *Theogony.*
9. Virgil, *Aeneid* 8.1.319ff.

A second stage follows in which the figure of Kronos takes on its central characteristic: placed between heaven and earth (his parents) he becomes an independent being, contradictory, dangerous and problematic. He generates sons who are destined to deprive him of the power he has conquered. He had experienced in the first stage the severe test of a father who prevented his liberation from the fertile and enveloping womb, and against that obstacle he had turned the unmeasurable violence of his thirst for liberty. Now he himself is threatened by that same force and violence, born as inevitable consequence of his life and destiny. This stage we can call the conservative stage.

In the first and second stages, the story of Kronos is essentially constituted by a father-son relationship of mutual competition, challenge, and violence. As in the first stage Kronos endures the hardness of the selfish father, so in the second stage he himself is the father who is frightened by the possibilities of his sons, and he, too, turns to deceit and violence in order to survive and keep his power.

In the third stage, we see the breakdown of this dramatic figure: he is deprived of his reign and while the generation of the Olympic gods begins, Kronos turns to the other side of his destiny. We see him now as king over a land very different from the titanic battlefield. The nature of the god is transformed: he is the wise and beneficent sovereign of happy men; the earth produces her goods in abundance; men and animals live in harmony.

According to another tradition, again referred to by Hesiod, Kronos, after being confined in the depths of the earth, sends beneficent spirits to men, making them capable of wise resolutions. This third stage we can call the "transformation."

We can now try to gain a better understanding of the archetype of Kronos-Saturn, amplifying its contents by the elements we find in other contexts. In the hermetic tradition, one speaks explicitly about Saturn, also in astrology, alchemy and in folklore. In the hermetic tradition Saturn, the planet whose orbit is the largest, corresponds to reason—or better, to the intellect in the non-rationalistic sense of the Greek "nous," which is a faculty of knowing by giving unity and shape to the object, the *principium individuationis* in the scholastic sense. (For the neo-Platonic Academy of Florence the etymology of Saturn was *sacer nous*, holy mind.)

Among the metals, Saturn is lead, the dark and heavy beginning in the scale of values toward gold. In the most ancient representation of the zodiac, every planet has two houses situated at the same level on both sides of a double course, first descending and then ascending. Saturn occupies the house at the lowest point, where descent ends and ascent be-gins. Here Saturn corresponds to the night sun; it is the winter solstice, the place of darkness and death. His symbol represents the sickle of the moon in the lowest position with respect to the cross. In terms of consciousness this corresponds to a state of chaotic submersion in the body. On the other hand, the "transformation," the changing from descent to ascent, occurs really in the house of Saturn. The life of sun and gold is hidden in the deep and obscure chaos of lead, where light and warmth seem to extinguish.

In the alchemical myth, the King Gold must be killed and buried in order to be able to rise again in his full glory, and it is precisely in the house of Saturn that he is buried. The tomb of the king is therefore called Saturn. The adept must complete a journey in order to have the revelation of hermetic wisdom. The starting point of the journey is the most westward of the seven mouths of the Nile, and there lives Saturn—the coldest, heaviest, and farthest from the sun, the planet symbolizing obscurity, melancholy, abandonment, and fear, the star of bad omen, the mysterious and sinister senex—they all transform upon arrival in *domus barbae*, the house where the "wisest of all," Hermes (Trismegistos), "three times the greatest," imparts wisdom.

In the transformation process of alchemy the first stage, which is dominated by Saturn, corresponds to the blackening and darkening, to the *putrefactio* and *mortificatio*. Grey and black are Saturn's colors, but the ashes that remain after the burning, the calcination of the base metals, the raw material, are also the precious material, the sediment from which afterward gold will be obtained. It will be the *sal sapientiae* or *Sal Saturni*, the bitter salt of wisdom, which makes undrinkable, though limpid, the water of life, the *aqua permanens*. This is the tincture, the womb of the *filius philosophorum*, that longed-for heavenly substance.

Titus Burckhardt, in his commentary on this first stage of magisterium, says:

> At the beginning of the spiritual realization stands death, in the
> form of "dying to the world." Consciousness must be withdrawn

from the senses and turned inward. As the "inner light" has not
yet risen, this turning away from the outward world is experienced as a *nox profunda* [deep dark night].[10]

Christian mysticism compares this state with the grain of corn,
which for fructifying must remain in the earth and die. Saturn is also
called by alchemists "the governor of the prison," the man who has the
power to keep imprisoned or to set free; he is the supreme judge.

In astrology, Saturn is the master of the sign of Capricorn; he is
characterized by the qualities of profundity, austerity, and renunciation, by pessimism, diffidence and selfishness. Saturn is represented as
an old man with a white beard and white hair, often with signs of bodily
infirmity, brandishing the sickle and the hourglass. He corresponds to
the "father" or to an important and aged person. Many of his characteristics tend toward a single point: a passionate concern, deep and continuous, in his own destiny, which may be manifested as concentration and
forbearance in duty, or as exhausting doubts and introspection about
the duty itself, as envy, mistrust, bad temper or hypochondria. Saturn
represents the driving power of the action that urges man to fulfill his
own destiny; he is the tendency toward thorough examination of his
own thoughts and feelings, continually dissecting his own actions, tor-
menting without rest himself and others. But Capricorn is also the sign
of wisdom and spiritual perseverance, of the capacity of renunciation,
austerity, and concentration.

Saturn is also the master of the sign that follows Capricorn—i.e.,
Aquarius, which means astrologically possible transformation toward
socially positive values, of humanitarianism and universal brother-
hood. This fact reminds us of the last stage of the myth of Saturn: the
Golden Age.

In fairy tales, we often encounter the figure of the old man. He is
the "wise old man," or the "wizard," or the "spirit of the mountain" who
lives in a castle or in a cave. He has an ambiguous nature and a surpris-
ing capacity for transformation. In some fairy tales, this ambiguous and
transforming nature is expressed by the fact that the old man has only
one side—one eye, one leg, one hand—the other side being invisible,

---

10. Titus Burckhardt, *Alchemy: Science of the Cosmos, Science of the Soul,* translated
by William Stoddart (Baltimore: Penguin Book, 1971), 186.

and revealing the old man's antithetical nature. He plays the role of the helper or the enemy, or a young man on his way to become a "hero," and also the role of the father or the one who holds imprisoned the princess for whom the "hero" is destined.[11]

As Jung says:

> The old man always appears when the hero is in a hopeless and desperate situation from which only profound reflection or a lucky idea—in other words, a spiritual function or an endo-psychic automatism of some kind—can extricate him. [This appearance is...] a purposeful process whose aim is to gather the assets of the whole personality together at the critical moment, when all one's spiritual and physical forces are challenged, and with this united strength to fling open the door of the future. No one can help the boy to do this; he has to rely entirely on himself. There is no going back. This realization will give the necessary resolution to his actions. By forcing him to face the issue, the old man saves him the trouble of making up his mind. Indeed the old man is himself this purposeful reflection and concentration of moral and physical forces that comes about spontaneously in the psychic space outside consciousness when conscious thought is not yet—or is no longer—possible.[12]

But "the old man has a wicked aspect too, just as the primitive medicine-man is a healer and helper and also the dreaded concocter of poisons."[13] He is "a helper, but also the contriver of a dangerous fate which might just as easily have turned out for the bad."[14] "He is a murderer...he is accused of enchanting a whole city by turning it to iron, i.e., making it immovable, rigid, and locked-up."[15]

On account of his role of keeper of the princess, "the fateful archetype of the old man has taken possession of the King's anima—in other words, robbed him of the archetype of life that the anima personifies—and forced him to go in search of the lost charm, the "treasure hard to attain," thus making him the mythical hero, the higher personality who

---

11. C. G. Jung, "The Phenomenology of Spirit in Fairytales," in *CW* 9.1, passim.
12. Ibid., §401–2.
13. Ibid., §414.
14. Ibid., §416.
15. Ibid., §417.

is an expression of the self. Meanwhile, the old man acts the part of the villain and has to be forcibly removed."[16] "So...we see the archetype of the old man in the guise of an evil-doer, caught up in all the twists and turns of an individuation process that ends suggestively with the *hieros gamos*,"[17] the sacred marriage.

CHARACTERISTICS OF THE KRONOS-SATURN ARCHETYPE

As will be said more extensively later, speaking about an archetype is not a harmless affair. We always risk losing its meaning if we try just to explain it, as if it were a rational or mechanical construction. We have to content ourselves with a description. But, to quote Jung, "The ultimate core of meaning (of an archetype] may be circumscribed, but not described. Even so, the bare circumscription denotes an essential step forward in our knowledge."[18] We should not forget to consider the peculiar characteristics of the archetype, not as definite concepts, but as images rich in emotional content and never isolated from their inter-relationship. Let us try therefore to outline the common structural nucleus, the active archetype, in all these expressions and human creations that explicitly refer to the image of Kronos-Saturn.

The Greek myth refers to an elementary and primeval aspect of endo-psychic development: the father-son relationship. Kronos is first the son who is prevented by the father from coming out of the mother's body; then he is the murderer of his father; then he himself is the father who swallows his own sons.

The entire story of Kronos seems guided by the leitmotif of his dogged search for and defense of his own individuality. This dramatic aspect is that which distinguishes Kronos from the other gods—from the Olympians, for instance, whose attributes are defined right from the beginning.

The risks Kronos runs are basically those of death: in the first stage, a death in the form of non-birth, of being prevented from being born; in the second stage, a death as loss of himself. In both cases, the threat of death enters into the father-son relationship, and the murderer is

---

16. Ibid., §418.
17. Ibid.
18. *CW* 9.1, §417.

always Kronos, who kills always in self-defense. There is a fundamental and absolute antagonism between these father and son aspects, for existence splits them apart. The dominant feeling is an unbearable yet unavoidable presentiment of death. Depression and anguish are recognizable in the hermetic and alchemic processes as the condition of gold hidden and imprisoned within lead, of the sun within the dark bowels of night, of burial within the earth, which means tomb and putrefaction, ignorance, obscurity and abandonment.

The potentiality of transformation is also evident in the alchemic as well as hermetic tradition. Saturn is the lowest point of the parabola, the most profound seat where the descent ends and the re-ascent begins. The direction is inverted, the meaning of his being is transformed: descent becomes the possibility for re-ascent, burial becomes contact with the fertile and profound womb of the night, depth becomes possibility for wisdom, putrefaction becomes liberation from death. That which is dead breaks down and dissolves, freeing the precious element that before was bound with an impure one.

The father-son conflict of Kronos says, in the incomparable way of mythical images, what philosophers have expressed in their abstract language as the essential dynamic of being and becoming. The old generates the new. But this continuity does not happen peacefully, because the old experiences the transformation as a threat, to which he reacts by swallowing every new offspring. The "new" revolutionary forces oppose this reactionary and conservative phase in a confrontation without compromise: one of the two must die, and the winner will reign. Hermetically Kronos-Saturn is the highest tester, the trial to be overcome, the governor of the prison in whose hands is liberation or confinement.

Another important aspect of the saturnic depression is the inhibition of will. It is neither a lack nor a primitive weakness of will, but a block provoked by an encounter with a contrary and more powerful will. If we look beneath the surface of psychotic melancholy, it is not a matter of an extinction of the will (as for instance seems to happen in catatonic schizophrenia), but rather an impossibility to get free from the snarls and obstacles that hinder, a wracking of one's brains about possible ways out, and a continuous collision with a greater and stronger obstacle. It is the condition of being swallowed and buried, just as happens to the sons of Kronos, or to gold in the stage of lead, or to the king in the tomb. Just as water becomes petrified in ice, so the cold and dry Saturn stops the movement and spontaneous flowing of the will. In the depressive phase of manic-depressive psychosis it often seems that the incessant activity of the manic phase is reversed toward the inside; and here it is feverishly manifested as an exaggerated lucidity in perceiving the negative aspects of existence and foreseeing damage and sorrow as inevitable developments of the present.

It may be said that saturnic inhibition is the fruit of an excess of awareness, of a harmful lucidity that paralyzes every step forward by the vision of a catastrophic and terrible failure. But the anxiety that derives from it is also a consequence of the fact that the subject does not perish, but witnesses with lucidity his continuous perishing. An extreme type of psychiatric melancholy shows these characteristics in their pure state. It is the Cotard syndrome,[19] which is fairly frequent in involutive forms of melancholy. It begins with transformation ideas; the subject feels his body in a state of decomposition, noted as a petrification of his organs. Then the idea of negation, in which the patient expresses a monstrous and terrible experience: he is no longer alive, and yet he will not be able to die, and he feels destined in eternity to witness his death and dissolution.

The melancholic inactivity joins with an interior hyperactivity, blocked in its possibilities of manifestation. It is not to be considered a contradiction, therefore, if in folklore we find in the large family of the sons of Saturn[20] men who continuously strive for repairing and contrive as artisans and farm workers, carpenters and shoemakers, tailors and masons, artists and poets. This motif of continuous work (though often not visible) approaches and overlaps the already considered motifs of drive toward transformation and individuation.

The meaning of being swallowed by the father, which is a constant of the saturnic psychology, may be explained as the blocking of an urge toward transformation. It is an archetypal expression for a peculiar moment in the process of the ego toward differentiation. Here the "hardened"—that is, all that has been already done, the established powers,

---

19. Henri Ey, *Études psychiatriques*, 3 vols. (Paris: Desclée de Brouwer, 1954).

20. Raymond Klibansky, Erwin Panofsky, and Fritz Saxl, *Saturn and Melancholy: Studies in the History of Natural Philosophy, Religion, and Art* (New York: Basic Books, 1966), 204–9, 217–20.

"history," impedes the drive of the youth toward the chances of the future; and the fascinating but regressive "chances of the past," linked with the realm of the mother, emerge from the darkness.

This state shows an exaggeration of awareness, of mental lucidity, of perfection in accomplishment. The power for which puer is longing is already possessed; the experience that he desires has already been experienced; the truth he seeks is already known. Kronos shows his unpleasant senex face to the juvenes, and the latter feels the urgency to cast aside all that the father has done. Springing with the freshness of mourning from the maternal womb, and directed with determination toward the process and the transformation, the protagonist meets the rigid figure of Kronos, unavoidable and contrary as death.

Another side we can look at, continuing this circumambulation of the figure of Kronos, is the omnipresent awareness of death. Death accompanies the various stages of the process as an inevitable counterpoint; there is no transformation without it. Among the characters participating in the tragic drama of the development of consciousness, there seems no possibility for agreement but through the death of one of the opponents. Every victory and affirmation of one must correspond to the defeat and death of the other. Father and son see reflected in each other what is in store for them—unavoidable old-age and decadence for the youth, confiscation, and discredit for the old.

In clinical manifestations of melancholic psychosis there is very often a delirium of guilt. A sense of guilt is hidden in the thoughts of the melancholic philosophers, in the passionate impetus of mystics. Kronos is dominated by a "bad conscience." He has earned existence at the price of his father's murder and the violent splitting of the undifferentiated unity of his parents. It is the original sin that religion and existential philosophy speak about. In the hermetic and alchemic tradition, this guilt is the impurity of the co-mingling of the precious element with ashes, earth and lead. The impurity reveals itself as original guilt, to the extent that it is negation and absence of the final state toward which the whole process aims.

The revolutionary need for new values must suffer and overcome, or go through the phase of opposition to, the established values, which makes for the guilt in every process of transformation of the new toward the old. But there is also the obscure guilt of the old toward the new, because the old knows he must succumb and that his being and doing contradict this superior law of transformation. Psychologically, it seems that guilt accompanies a certain phase in every transformation process, in which one aspect of guilt will join others: the need for transformation, the inhibition of the will, the awareness of death. The necessity for transformation seems a fundamental threat to present being, for the "horizon" of the ego is bound to its present identifications and nonetheless obliged to change.

Guilt is psychologically bound to punishment, to the feeling of being in the hands of a power that can destroy. For the son this power is Kronos, the old king, the negative father. Kronos-Saturn is the archetype of the test one must pass, the person with whom you must settle the account, whose place you must take. He is bigger, wiser, more powerful, and the fear of facing him causes a stop in the transformation process and a stagnation of libido, but also an increase of endo-psychic tension.

In speaking about Hermes-Mercury in alchemy and hermetics, Jung says that the ambivalent nature of this figure may be considered as a "process" that begins with evil and ends with good. Saturn, he says, represents the evil side that is contained in Mercury. In his work on the Spirit-Mercury, Jung says also that the *principium individuationis* may be seen as the spirit that has been confined and imprisoned. He who has imprisoned is "the Lord of Souls," but he did so with good intentions, for only through the sense of guilt that arises from the separation of good and bad can the moral conscience be developed. He says, "Since without guilt there is no moral consciousness...we must concede that the strange intervention of the master of souls was absolutely necessary for the development of any type of consciousness and in this sense was for the good."[21] In the same work, Jung reminds us that for pessimistic philosophy, as for Schopenhauer and for Buddhism, the principle of individuation is the source of every ill. So Kronos-Saturn, the star of depression, separation, moral suffering, guilt, master of the prison, represents the necessary negative moment of the individuation process.

In the *Mysterium Coniunctionis,* Jung expresses the moment in which guilt reveals its positive possibility: "Only then will he realize that the conflict is in him, that the discord and tribulation are his riches, which

---

21. *CW*13, §244.

should not be squandered by attacking others; and that, if fate should exact a debt from him in the form of guilt, it is a debt to himself."[22]

But Kronos-Saturn becomes the god of agriculture, who reigns over men and teaches them the arts of cultivation, only when he has been knocked down and forced to vomit his swallowed sons. The seed that dies is that which fructifies; the sickle, symbol of death, becomes the tool that harvests fruit and nourishment.

In the ancient representations of the Zodiac, Saturn is the lowest and final point of descent. Therefore, it is the negative pole toward which we must direct ourselves in order to be able to turn toward the positive pole. In other words, it is to seek darkness, pain, death, to be able to re-ascend into light, joy and life. The astrological symbol of Saturn has the shape of a sickle, the waning moon, at the lowest point of the cross; it is the place of death *for* transformation, which is the meaning of sacrifice.

Also in the alchemical process the king must be killed in order to arise again in glory. He is buried in the house of Saturn, which has the double significance of tomb, where the old decays, and the seed that prepares the new birth is contained. An Orphic hymn to Kronos speaks to the god: "You consume all things/and replenish them too."[23]

At the end of his story, Kronos-Saturn, with his last transformation, seems to go beyond time, thereby disclosing the full meaning of his process. According to the tradition handed down by Hesiod, Kronos reigns over the men of the Golden Age, who lived without worry, effort or complaint, as gods. The misery of old age did not threaten them; with bodies eternally young, they enjoyed their feasts free of ill. They died as if overcome by sleep. Every good was available to them: the fields, givers of life, produced their fruits in great abundance. They lived gladly from such fruits in peace, in a community composed entirely of good people. They were rich in flocks and were friends of the blessed gods. When this generation sank, by the will of Zeus, into the hidden depths of the earth, they became the good spirits that moved about the earth as protectors of men, defenders of justice, givers of wealth, invisibly present everywhere.

---

22. *CW* 14, §511ff.

23. "To Kronos," in *The Orphic Hymns*, translated by Apostolos N. Athanassakis and Benjamin M. Wolkow (Baltimore: Johns Hopkins University Press, 2013), 15.

Hesiod also tells that Kronos, after his dethronement, is appointed by Zeus to govern the islands of the blessed; at the end of the world, surrounded by the ocean, these islands are inhabited by heroes after their death. There the fertile fields bear fruit three times a year, "honey drips from the oak trees." This is the last transformation of the Titanic devourer of his sons; now he is friend of men and guides them on paths of peace and love. In terms of the anima, all the qualities that character-ize this phase of the reign of Kronos are the gifts that wisdom brings to men. Wisdom, which is creative possibility because it discloses interior wealth, is also justice, because it is the capacity of unity and harmony between contrary forces and needs.

The analysis of depression, dominated by the ambiguous symbol of the old man with the sickle, brings us therefore to a dynamic nucleus of the collective psyche. We can try to circumscribe this nucleus by bipolar images or concepts of opposites - such as death and eternal life, chaos and wisdom (for Gnostics Saturn is the son of Chaos!), impurity and purity, petrification and transformation, confusion and lucidity, guilt and glorification, punishment and reward, torment as mere suffering and sacrifice, sterile poverty and fertile wealth, violent opposition and the harmony of justice.

CORRELATIONS AND DYNAMICS OF THE KRONOS–SATURN ARCHETYPAL FIELD

In the same manner as forces from different fields meet to create a com-plex field of energy, we can notice other archetypes converging upon that of the old man. Also, as one cannot try to describe the function of an organ without being compelled, at a certain point, to cross over into the function of another organ, so it is that the Kronos-Saturn figure is in part superimposed upon and joined with other archetypes. These analogies with the physical concept of "field" and with the physiologi-cal concept of "organ" perhaps help better to understand the real state of affairs in the world of the collective unconscious.

When one inquires thoroughly enough into an archetype, one reaches the moment in which the figure fades and, gradually losing its clear outlines, dissolves into other closely related figures, which seem to aid in understanding but at the same time deprive the original arche-type of its singular value. Every archetype seems clarified when we discover its vital connection with other archetypes, but in so doing it is dismembered by and dissolves into the others. This is especially evident when inquiring into that totality of the self, the supra-ordinate personality. Here, we cannot affirm anything of the archetype in itself, except that which is manifested by the images of dreams, myths, fantasy, etc. We cannot help but approach these psychic elements first with our intuitive and affective faculties, and then more and more with our thinking, since we no longer naively experience the myth, but want to be scientific in our attitude. Our analysis, however, does not find an end. As soon as we try to abstract the very essence of the archetypal image, it fades and evaporates. Only the image itself, presented in its usual context, is clear, perspicuous, and unequivocal.[24] The main experience we have in studying an archetype is not only its infinite possibility to be analyzed, but also the loss of its singularity and individuality. We perceive the fundamental relationship with other archetypes; we discover the underground identifications between opposites, and the ever present dialectical structure between them. Therefore, we should always, when facing the difficult task of speaking about an archetype, refer first to the fundamental lines of relationship with neighboring archetypes, and second, to their transformation in the individuation process.

With this in mind, we turn again to Saturn, where we find two other archetypes related directly to him. Inasmuch as Saturn is the old man, he unites with and opposes puer. Inasmuch as he is the father, he unites with and opposes the mother. Puer and senex are the personifications of the two extremes into which the libido in a certain condition splits. In the old man the process has stopped in an excess of egocentric differentiation, which has exhausted the transformation potential; it has become petrified, and the old man, detaining the power, tends to block and petrify the process around him. By now Kronos is hardened by his thirst for power and by his fear of what is new. The youth represents the need to become the new man, but can achieve this only to the extent that he collides with the petrified wall of the senex. The two archetypes are the poles of a singular dynamic aspect.

The archetype of the mother is in mutual relationship with the father (Mythology, alchemy and hermetics are full of material in this

---

24. *CW* 9.1, §301.

regard). But the mother is also allied with the son in his struggle against the father, as is shown in the story of Kronos and repeatedly by alchemists. The mother is bound to puer in an energy-loaded relationship; but the positive or negative value of such relationship depends on how the father constellates. The negative father, the overwhelming test, the threatening opposition of the rival castled in his established power, the hardened parent as a judge—provoke the withdrawal of puer toward the all-understanding mother and her infinite capacity for transformation as the undifferentiated Great Mother. So puer's drive toward the future is stopped and is compelled to reverse its course. This is the leitmotif of the tendency toward death, which is one aspect of puer. Certainly it is a death essentially different from that which is threatened by the father-devourer, a death this time not feared but desired, ecstatic suicide and dissolution.

The clinical manifestations of melancholy do not lack concrete examples of this aspect of the archetype: on the one hand, the fear of guilt and punishment and, on the other, the desire for death as a way out. In adolescent depression one may see expressed an ambivalent link with the mother; she would be seen as a protective refuge against the threatening and excessive demands of the father, while the father as *principium individuationis* would be felt as a threat because he seems to represent the loss of contact with the infinite possibilities of the mother. In this case, the mother would be only a pseudo-positive figure, because she herself now represents the petrification of the process. She carries now the Saturn characteristics and thus becomes, in an ambiguous and deadly manner, the negative devouring mother.

But the mother contains also all the elements of the anima: inexhaustible richness of sentiment and emotion, fertility, creativity. She is the source of birth and rebirth, renewal, transmutation. The anima personalizes the mother and brings her to an individual level, and is therefore guide and connection to the unconscious.

When puer and senex collide irreducibly, the breakdown in the process may be overcome through the anima. Puer fears the old man precisely because puer feels in him the hardness and aridity that derive from the old man's lack of contact with eros, from the absence of instinct and creative emotion.

According to alchemists it is necessary that the hardened element be dissolved, dismembered, and buried in the primeval formless matter in order to be able to rise again as a new man. Naturally, this is feared by the old man, whose meaning is contrary to the formless, the mutable, the multiform, the not-yet-constituted and not individualized. He is the powerful drive of the libido toward definite forms—just what puer fears as death! One could say that puer and senex project their shadows upon each other. Let it be said in parentheses: this affirmation might be purely analogical, and could risk a certain confusion. "Shadow" must perhaps be said in reference to a person and "projection" to a personal relationship. But in treating the archetype, every archetypal personification has a shadow *sui generis*, which might be appropriately called Syzygy, a term that Jung has taken from astrology. It means the positions of the moon in junction or in opposition to the sun; astrologically speaking, Syzygy has the significance of a couple yoked together.

The mixture of the personal sphere with that of the archetypical can lead the Jungian student into dangerous confusion; it is advisable not to waste any of the precious possibility for clarification when one deals with a field so complex and difficult to grasp.

The resolution of the puer-senex conflict can be found in the mediating function of the anima. In the myth of Kronos the resolution is the transformation of Kronos-Saturn into the God of Agriculture, founder and ruler of the Golden Age, or Lord of the Tartars and sender of good spirits. Here the relation with the feminine is fundamental, for the old man must be dissolved. In the everlasting process of transformation, every completed form must decay, every conquered power must be lost, everything born must die.

The senex can signify that the process has stopped, that the subject has not had the courage to sacrifice what has been conquered and doesn't trust the mysterious and antithetic regenerating power of the formless, the unconscious, whose messenger is the anima.

For puer it is not a matter of withdrawing himself from the influence of the old man, nor of opposing him. This would be impossible if we reflect that puer and senex, syzygial aspects of the archetype, are born one from the other! Puer must accept his own death, and that is the meaning of his collision with the old man. The youth has just been born and still carries with him the fascinating memory of the infinite, immortal depth of the mother. He has no form, but unlimited possibilities. He fears every form like death. Such an attitude is peculiar to "puer aeternus," since the "changeling" wants to remain such and not take only one form. But when the unavoidable necessity of existence compels puer to take a form, the struggle with senex, the negative father, begins. That is the *principium individuationis* as "puer aeternus" experiences it. The unconscious suicidal tendency is nothing but the strong drive toward transformation, which is an essential constituent of puer. Death has for puer the desperate and terrifying aspect of the old man with the sickle, or as an alternative, the fascinating realm of the mother. But the "bitter cup" that is offered by the father is also the potion that can transform the youth into hero. Death itself can therefore be transformed into "a death of what I am now in order to become what I want to be!" Transformation and redemption by sacrifice are the calling of puer. The unifying symbol and redeeming personification that can arise now for him is just that of kore or anima. She acts as mediator between the needs that the old man imposes and the values that the mother represents.

In fairy tales, if the youth accepts the sacrifice that is the struggle and the risk of death (in fact the youth always dies in the struggle, but to arise transformed), then having won, he can marry the daughter of the old king—the young anima, the eternal creative possibility contained as Sophia in the old man who dissolves. This marriage with the daughter of the old king may be compared with the agricultural or Golden Age of Kronos-Saturn, when he sends inspiring spirits from the underground.

John Pordage, the English alchemist cited by Jung in "The Psychology of the Transference," says concerning the "opus:"

> ...the delicate Tincture, this tender child of life,...must descend into the darkness of Saturn, wherein no light of life is to be seen; there it must be held captive, and be bound with the chains of darkness...

But, he continues,

> ...in the darkness of this black is hidden the light of lights in the quality of Saturn...the Tincture of Life is in this putrefaction or dissolution and destruction...You must not despise this blackness, or black colour, but persevere in it in patience, in suffering, and in silence,...until the days of its tribulations are completed, when the seed of life shall waken to life, shall rise up, sublimate or glorify itself, transform itself into whiteness, purify and sanctify itself...When the work is brought thus far, it is an easy work: for

the learned philosophers have said that the making of the stone is then woman's work and child's play.

And about the ultimate stage of the process he says,

>...then you will see the beginning of its resurrection from hell, death, and the mortal grave, appearing first in the quality of Venus;...and the gentle love-fire of Venus quality will gain the upper hand, and the love-fire Tincture will be preferred in the government and have supreme command. And then the gentleness and love-fire of Divine Venus will reign as lord and king in and over all qualities.[25]

In the final stage, the opus has therefore gained a purified and bright space, in which the archetype of the anima appears. Meister Eckhart says:

>So in the heaven of the soul Saturn is a cleanser giving angelic purity and brings about vision of the godhead; as our Lord said, "blessed are the pure in heart, for they shall see God."[26]

In psychological terms, one would say that the old man uses the function of anima as a link between the unconscious and the conscious ego This connection has the power of inspiring good decisions, positive and concrete actions. It is the peculiar power of Sophia or of Athena, the daughter born from her father's head.

This final synthesis between the masculine and feminine is also seen in the Hermaphroditus, as the alchemists call the final work of the pro-cess. In regard to this Jung quotes a German poem written in the first half of the sixteenth century, in which the nature of the Hermaphroditus is explained. In the poem the queen speaks as follows:

>Then it was that I first knew my son/
>and we two came together as one.
>There I was made pregnant by him and gave birth
>Upon a barren stretch of earth.
>I became a mother and remained a maid/
>And in my nature was established.
>Therefore my son was also my father /
>As God ordained in accordance with nature.[27]

---

25. Cited in *CW* 16, §§510–13.
26. Cited in Klibansky, et al., *Saturn and Melancholy*, 168.
27. *CW* 16, §528.

Also in Zosimos: "Its (the stone's) mother is a virgin, and the father lay not with her."[28] Then Petrus Bonus in *Theatrum chemicum*:

> Whose mother is a virgin and whose father knew not woman...God must become man, because on the last day of this art, when the completion of the work takes place, begetter and begotten become altogether one. Old man and youth, father and son, become altogether one. Thus all things old are made new.[29]

This may throw some light on the destiny of old man and youth in this final stage.

As we have seen, it is not possible to describe this Kronos-Saturn aspect without mention of the essential syzygial aspects of puer and mother, and without arriving at kore as correlative of the last transformation. For the sake of exposition, we can describe this journey as passing through three phases. In the first phase consciousness is formed as that function of knowing that acts only whenever there is a separation of and tension between polarities. This is the "birth" of the ego and of knowledge. From this point on, the story of the ego will be characterized by two relationships: one with a *Mater*, from whom he must go out, unfold, grow up, express himself; another with a *Pater*, to whom he must give account and who is force and resistance to conquer, an obstacle to be overcome, a test to be accepted. These two relationships are the same that in other schools of psychology are called, perhaps in a more static and dogmatic way, pleasure principle and power principle, or Id and Super-Ego.

In the second phase of the movement of the ego toward the self, there is represented the "becoming" of the consciousness. Kronos is swallowed by the father. Here, too, the protagonist is "shut up," "inside," held in the belly—but what may be the meaning that this happens now inside the father? Is it a question of the, "awareness of being swallowed," or of the state of being inside looking for the possibility of getting out?

While being swallowed into the mother is more similar to the infantile unconsciousness, and perhaps to certain forms of quiet stupor in psychiatric pathology, the second type, being swallowed into the father, well describes the grief of the melancholic person. This grief can also be

---

28. *Artis auriferae*; cited in *CW* 16, §529n.10.
29. Cited in *CW* 16, §529n.11.

seen as a kind of mania reversed, introverted and inhibited, a terrible lucidity and awareness of one's own condition.

We have already mentioned the Cotard syndrome of psychotic invasion of the archetype. It might be worthwhile to quote a poem of the Italian poetess Ada Negri, which impressively expresses the same condition:

ANNIVERSARY

Don't call me, don't tell me anything
Don't try to make me smile.
Today I'm like a wild beast
That has shut himself up to die.

Turn down the light, cover the fire,
That the room be like a tomb.
Let me huddle in the corner
With my head on my knees.

Let the hours extinguish in silence
Let the torpid waves of anxiety
Rise up and drown me;
I ask nothing but to lose consciousness.

But it isn't granted to me.
That face, that smile
Are always before me
Day and night memory is a hook
Fixed in my living flesh.

Perhaps I will never be able to die:
Condemned in eternity
To keep vigil of the havoc within me,
Crying with lid-less eyes.[30]

Consciousness of being buried, in philosophical terms, is the paradoxical experience of death peculiar to man. Of death itself we cannot have experience, yet it constitutes the dominating thought, the background against which we perceive life. It is just in this being buried that man seems enriched by his most original and profound values. Precisely because he realizes the meaninglessness and formlessness of life, he can find the tension that makes possible his creative life.

---

30. "Anniversario," in Ada Negri, *Il libro di Mara* (Milan: Fratelli Treves Editori, 1919), 57–58; my translation.

Kronos-Saturn, the negative father, constellates within the unconscious as the devouring father at the moment in which there is formed
in the personality the drive to grow up, toward individuation. It is the
moment when the subject feels swallowed by collective forms, laws,
customs, systems. The swallowing by the father may present a variety
of aspects, but in general it has to do with conscious depression, an
abaissement du niveau mental together with lucid presence. Jung uses
the concept of regression in a similar manner.

> The hero is the symbolical exponent of the movement of libido.
> Entry into the dragon is the regressive direction, and the jour-
> ney to the East (the "night sea journey")...symbolizes the effort to
> adapt to the conditions of the psychic inner world...
>
> It is characteristic that the monster begins the night sea jour-
> ney to the East, i.e., towards sunrise, while the hero is engulfed in
> its belly. This seems to me to indicate that regression is not nec-
> essarily a retrograde step in the sense of a backwards develop-
> ment or degeneration, but rather represents a necessary phase of
> development. The individual is, however, not consciously aware
> that he is developing; he feels himself to be in a compulsive situa-
> tion that resembles an early infantile state or even an embryonic
> condition within the womb.[31]

This womb can as well be the father's belly—in which case, the ego, being
differentiated from the mother, is conscious of its confinement. The state
may coincide with the phase of the hero myth that Neumann defines
as "patriarchal castration," characterized by compulsory spiritual life[32]
as well as with those archetypal motifs in which a rational intellectual
power acts to the rigorous exclusion of every irrational function.

At this point it might be useful to refer to a dream of a patient suffering from depressive psychosis, a recurring dream that always came
some days before the beginning of the psychotic crisis. In the dream the
patient relived his experience as a prisoner of war. *He found himself in a
stone quarry in the concentration camp at Mauthausen. He knew that the
war was over, but he could not leave the camp.* The dream, with its power
of synthesis, contains many elements found in the archetypal structure

---

31. *CW* 8, §§68–69.

32. Erich Neumann, *The Origins and History of Consciousness*, translated by R. F. C.
Hull (New York: Pantheon Books, 1954), 187.

of melancholy. The stone quarry is a saturnic engulfment that as a hostile and violent power, holds the subject prisoner. In his painful impotence, the patient recognized the awakening of an autonomous force, an archetype, compelling him to such a condition.

After about a year, during which the patient had undergone psychological treatment, he had once more a depressive crisis. This time the dream was somewhat different: *the prisoner was again in the quarry, although the war was over. A young unknown woman appeared and the two of them weaved in and out of the quarry until the prisoner suddenly realized that in fact one could go out! But as he was about to escape, the thought came to him that they might by way of retaliation do harm to his mother. Still, he left the quarry, hoping to be able to notify her in time.* The possibility of liberation is linked with the appearance of the anima. The patient's affect, representing his deeper unconscious layer, is still bound to the mother, and therefore still exposed to the enemy.

"Man cannot be described but as antinomies," Jung reminds us. In his "Psychology of the Transference" and *Mysterium Coniunctionis,* Jung has described the dynamic correlations, direct and crossing, between the four persons of the "marriage quaternio."[33] In its original alchemical aspect, this *quaternio* was composed of king, queen, adept and *soror mystica.* Such dynamic correlations risk seeming too entangled, but, as a matter of fact, they correspond to a few fundamental rules of analytical psychology: the complementary and compensatory relation between the conscious and the unconscious; the bipolarity of the archetypes; the different attitudes of the individual toward archetypes and external world—identity, identification, projection, introjection, integration—the possibility that the transference relationship occurs by means of the conscious aspect of one partner and the unconscious of the other, or by means of the unconscious of both.

When an archetype constellates, a bipolar field is formed. In this case, for example, the appearance of senex must give rise to the appearance of puer, just as in physics "every action has an equal and contrary reaction." Generally, this bipolar field will be experienced by the conscious mind as an inescapable alternative. As we have seen, the opposition within the Syzygy is in itself unsolvable, *tertium non datur.* In our

---

33. Cf. *CW*16, §§425ff.; *CW*14, §§1ff.;

case, there are only two alternatives for the subject: the identification with senex, with his propensity for law and order and rigid form. He will then naturally project the image of puer on "others"—the anarchists and revolutionaries, young people who want only to destroy and flee from every duty. Or else the subject will lean toward the identification with puer and his dramatic destiny. Then appearing in his story will be senex, whom he will see, by projection, in the external world—the egoism, jealousy, repression, lack of imagination of the elder generation.

If an archetypal image appears in the objective world of inter-personal relationships, it cannot remain without effect in the opposite field of introversion, of relationship with the unconscious. We have seen that when senex is projected into the outside world and the conscious ego identifies with puer, then the mother complex activates in the unconscious. It may be recalled that puer means the birth, from the mother or the unconscious, of a principle that is basically a need for development, change and transformation; this will be stopped against the opposite figure that means rigor, hardness, immutability, necessity of having a definite form. Then puer has a regression toward the mother, toward the regressive aspects of the mother; that is, involution, undifferentiation and death. This unconscious activation of the negative mother has a part in forming the shadow of puer—his melancholic aspect, unavoidable for him as a destiny.

Let us consider now the case in which the subject leans toward identification with senex, and the figure of puer appears projected in the outer world.

As confirmed by mythology, hermetics and fairy tales, as well as by psychological practice, there is a peculiar connection between senex and anima: she is prisoner, or in some way subject to the old man, king, wizard or chthonic godhead. It is this imprisoned anima that activates in the unconscious of a person who has let his personality slide under the archetype of senex. In the form of wizard, he becomes malicious, cunning, transformer, hot-tempered—all signs of a certain invasion by the anima.

This schematic explanation of the dialectical relationship between archetypes—between conscious and unconscious and between the external, or extroverted, reality and the internal, or introverted, reality—may help to understand a few interpersonal relations: for example, in the world of today, the collective collision between puer and senex, where each one identifies with one of the Syzygy and projects the other one. These correlations seem to be confirmed also by the subsequent events in the story of Kronos-Saturn. In that which we called the third phase there is the solution of the drama. According to their destiny of tragic characters, the two opposing protagonists must meet death: the old man, dissolution, according to the alchemical rule of being dissolved; puer, on his part, the sacrifice. But this encounter with death, this return to the mother is made possible by the appearance of a redeeming or demiurgic figure who achieves the transformation of Kronos-Saturn.

The new issue of Kronos is characterized by creativity, which is a positive relation with concreteness and objectivity as well as with inconstancy and wealth of possibility. There the two opposite values of senex and puer find an organic synthesis—or better, they transcend in a new form. The archetypal image that appears in this phase is for a man the anima. She represents the individual mediator with the world of the mother, a world that for senex and puer could only be that of death. But for the hero who *has known his own death,* who has experienced the dissolution and the *sacrifice,* who has faced the night sea journey or the underground descent, it is the encounter and marriage with the bride, a fertile joining between the opposites, individual creative activity.

The anima seems born of the unconscious and presents herself as a possibility to the ego as result of a tension toward individuation created and maintained by the constellating of puer and senex. That is the origin of what Jung calls a symbol—the images of the anima that in each case are presented as spontaneous products of the unconscious.

The peace among animals and men on earth is a sign of a state of inner harmony, consequence of a cosmic harmony; i.e., of archetypal forces of the collective unconscious. Heaven and earth, father and mother, are no longer in conflict; the mother is now the good earth, rich in fruits; the father is the god-king, or the god-protector of good laws. Men live in harmony with each other because they are in peace within themselves. The new man, born again in *novam infantiam,* the redeemed, the arisen, owes his own existence to the end of the war between the principle of power and the principle of transformation, between him who sets the limits and him who continuously breaks them. *Creativity* is the concept that expresses the unification of the two opposites.

EPILOGUE

The final state of harmony of that individuation process manifested in the story of Kronos-Saturn seems splendidly expressed by one of the most popular, though perhaps least understood, genre of Renaissance paintings—that Renaissance in which some of the most representative men chose the figure of Saturn as "father" and as "patron god," and during which the "sacred story" was often deeply experienced in the hermetic or alchemic spirit. I speak of the innumerable representations of the Madonna with child, often accompanied by holy figures. The one I choose as an example, and one could use many others, is the *Sacred Conversation* by Palma il Vecchio, which can be found in the Kunsthistorisches Museum in Vienna, painted at the beginning of the sixteenth century.

Near the old tree, probably where, according to the Christian holy story, the "process" and the primeval splitting of the contraries in the newborn consciousness of the first couple began, the Holy Mother and child form the new couple Man and Woman. The child is "the New Man," the *renovatum ad novam infantiam*, the "redeemer redeemed." The woman is the mother, but purified from every mortal co-mingling, and not touched in any way by the earthly father, by all that has passed, or by any possessions. She is the Virgin; she is purity itself at its source, the inexhaustible origin.

At their side, the two saints seem to be images of the two principal characters in the drama we spoke about: the old man and the youth in their irresolvable struggle. Melancholic persons doomed to death, desperate bearers of the cross, their faces express profound nostalgia or the bitter torment of search. The three-fold cross of the old man is certainly related to the puzzle of unity and trinity, the eternally disappointed intellect in its search for definite truth. The lamb of the youth reminds one of innocence and sacrifice. Beside every masculine figure there is a feminine one: the two young women whom the two characters of the drama do not yet seem to notice, immersed as they are in their sorrowful "passion," promise individual mediation with the mother; they seem personifications of the anima.

One seeks in vain traces of the Great Father in these holy conversations. On the other hand, the mother and child seem to form a couple completely self-sufficient. Perhaps the squared stone at the base, a very

Jacopo Negretti, called Palma il Vecchio
Sacred Conversation, c. 1520–22
Egg tempera on wood
Kunsthistorisches Museum Wien, Gemäldegalerie

saturnic sign, alludes to the beginning of the process. A key to understanding the relationship between the two is therefore offered by the knowledge that the Virgin is also "daughter of her son," and the "father" is in the child himself.

In effect, the old man, the father, is spread throughout the entire scene. His spirit hovers there—perhaps just because of his absence. But he is concretely present in the child as the potentiality of individuation, as *principium individuationis,* which rules without being a separate person. He is no longer in conflict with the mother because indeed he is continuously born from the mother, who is no more the undifferentiated *prima materia* but the inspiring Sophia or the anima—or, in the language of analytical psychology, the way to the Self, the "individuation process."

Thus seems to culminate the story of the old man, the negative father, who at the end reveals the positive possibility that is in him. Depression and melancholy can be seen as the face of the process in which the figure of the father constellates negatively. The more opposition to the archetype, the more powerful and destructive are his effects. From psychotic depressions to a neurotic restriction and fear of creativity to a depressive personality, the results of a wrong adjustment to the action of the Saturn archetype are expressed.

> We may long have known the meaning, effects, and characteristics of unconscious contents…The only way to get at them in practice is to try to attain a conscious attitude which allows the unconscious to co-operate instead of being driven into opposition.[34]

These words of Jung are the most suitable comment to the ultimate possibility of depression. When accepted, melancholy would become what Ficino called "generous melancholy." By accepting one's cosmic solitude, with its temporal and mortal destiny, and by overcoming its meaninglessness, one would discover the synthesis between two major and most compulsive and, at first glance, contrary psychic entities: the need for an ever-changing state of freedom that may endlessly "go beyond," and the need to block the stream of life in definite, concrete, and possibly imperishable forms.

---

34. *CW* 16, §366.

On the Father in Psychotherapy

VERA VAN DER HEYDT

Freud was very much concerned about the role the father plays, but he was particularly mindful of the negative castrating aspect of the father from the son's point of view, essential in the Victorian era. Jung wrote one short essay on the father: *The Significance of the Father in the Destiny of the Individual,* which was published in 1909; Jung revised it twice, the last time in 1948. This essay is important as Jung states in it his theory that the magical hold and influence parents have over their children is due not only to the personality of the individual parent but to the power of the archetype that stands behind them.

In later works, remarks about the personal father are scattered throughout Jung's writings; mainly, however, he examines the father-son relationship as it appears in mythology, in religion and in alchemy, and then he takes this archetypal relationship symbolically as an image from which the interdependence of self and ego in the individual psyche can be understood.

Jung's very particular attention was devoted to the mother and to her double role: life-giving and nourishing, and her destructive and devouring aspect. He was concerned to show how these two aspects belong to the archetypal mother—nature, matter—as can be seen in the figures of the mother goddesses all over the world and also appear in every individual woman. He stressed this aspect of life because the earth and the body, the mother world, had been repressed and diminished for centuries, particularly in the Christian world.

First presented to the Society of Analytical Psychology Club, London. An earlier version was published as "The Role of the Father in Early Mental Development" in the *British Journal of Medical Psychology 37* (1964).

What has happened since, however, is that mother, and in particular the personal mother and her role, seems to have been overemphasized to the point where all responsibility is laid at her door: all later neurotic trouble in the child is traced to a faulty relationship at the breast, and the role of mother is stressed almost as against the role of wife or the role of woman as a whole.

Not so long ago the father was the most important person of the family, and obedience was owed to him by his wife as well as by his children. He was the sole breadwinner; he was responsible for the welfare of his family, for education, choice of profession, etc. He also carried responsibility for the actions of his family.

Now the wife is the husband's equal economically and legally; mother's greater importance in the family unit has been proclaimed. Much of father's responsibility has been taken over by the Welfare State, and so father has been dethroned by both the mother and the State.

The Church used to uphold automatically the father's authority over his family, as being a reflection of the eternal authority of the Father who is in Heaven. The Church is more alive now to the dangers of such an identification: so, father has also been dethroned by the Church.

The father's status has changed therefore in the external world; he is no longer carried collectively as the predominant figure. This change has affected the individual father, making him insecure and uncertain as to his role in the family. Thus father tends to withdraw from the family leaving decisions to the "mother," thereby fatally strengthening her animus.

Furthermore, values that belong to the transpersonal father, to the father world, are questioned and attacked: law, order, discipline, self-control, morality, taking responsibility, having responsibility are all queried and even have been declared to be damaging to the individual's development. Other father-world values have also been at-tacked: for instance the courage of pilots, so it has been said, has to do with the negative side of the *puer aeternus*, with a compulsion to be flying in the clouds away from the reality of life; the courage needed for mountaineering, we are told, has something to do with a desire to overcome mother and trample on her breasts. Infantile motives and motivations are doubtless contained in all our actions, but there has been so much attention given to the negative shadow side—forgetting the body that casts it—in much psychological teaching that it has seeped through to the general attitude as "nothing but."

Bruno Bettelheim, the Austrian psychoanalyst who is now professor of educational psychology in the University of Chicago, was imprisoned in concentration camps for several years. In his book *The Informed Heart*, he describes his experiences and the conclusions he came to with regard to some aspects of psychoanalytic theory. I quote:

> While in camp, I was little concerned with whether psychoanalytic theory was adequate and only with the problem of how to survive in ways that would protect both my physical and moral existence. Therefore what struck me first was the realization that those persons who according to psychoanalytic theory as I understood then, should have stood up best under the rigor of the camp experience, were often very poor examples of human behavior under extreme stress. Others who, according to the same body of theory and the expectations based on it should have done poorly, presented shining examples of human courage and dignity...
>
> It would just not do under conditions prevailing in the camps to view courageous, life engendering actions as an outgrowth of the death instinct, aggression turned against self, testing the indestructibility of the body, megalomanic denial of danger, histrionic feeding of one's narcissism or whatever other category the action would have to be viewed from in psychoanalysis. These and many other interpretations have validity in terms of depth psychology or the psychology of the unconscious, and they certainly did apply. Only viewing courageous behavior by a prisoner within the spectrum of depth analysis seemed ludicrously beside the point. So while psychoanalysis lost nothing as far as it went, it went unexpectedly, and in terms of my expectations, shockingly short of the mark.[1]

The archetypal father has disappeared into the unconscious, is repressed. and is therefore causing disturbances, confusion and unpleasant symptoms. The personal father, according to reports by social workers, is also disappearing. In Britain and America, the high incidence of desertion, separation and divorce is remarked upon and

---

1. Bruno Bettelheim: *The Informed Heart: Autonomy in a Mass Age* (Glencoe, Ill.: The Free Press, 1960), 13–14, 17.

the effect this has on the mother and children; mother's anger and distress is felt by the children; a negative unreal image of the father is presented to them by the mother that is often strengthened by personal unfortunate experiences. A sense of shame is activated in the child for not having been able to hold father's affection, and also shame is felt for being 'different' from other children. As a consequence both a girl and a boy distrust the possibility of achieving a relationship with the opposite sex; the girl may be afraid of man for the rest of her life, and the boy finds it difficult to develop or trust his own masculine powers as the male ideal in the person of the father was destroyed.

These difficulties assailing the deserted mother and children have been noted for some time. Very rarely, however, does one find any mention of the problems of the husband-father that drove him away from his family. In America it seems that a high percentage of men left their families after the permanent arrival of their mothers-in-law in the home. A milder form of disappearance is experienced in our present-day society through the fact that father works so far from home that his family, certainly his children, hardly ever see him.

When the father's disappearance is occasioned by his death, particularly if he was a war hero, the mother may present an idealized unreal image of him to her children; in this case feelings of inadequacy and of guilt may arise in them because of the hopelessness of ever being able to be worthy of such a saint-like person.

In the beginning of life the child telescopes mother-father into one figure. In early children's drawings one can see sometimes a human figure with a penis that the child calls mother; father is an appendix of the mother—he is the penis. Gradually, as consciousness emerges, the child differentiates father from mother and recognizes him as a person in his own right, and mother as a person in hers; this is a completely new situation and one of the greatest significance.

The tremendous crisis and conflict in the life of every child with the possibilities of traumatic consequences, and in which love and loyalties are put to the test, appear in the Oedipal situation. Freud put this conflict around the age of three to five. Jung asserts that a child's essential characteristics have evolved by then, and that it is possible to foresee the kind of collisions there will be between the child and his parents later on. This implies that the child himself can be aware at that time of the differences between himself and his parents, and this may sharpen the inner conflict. Furthermore, it is at this time that a child is confronted with rivals in the form of siblings that can make a child feel rejected and deprived. It is understandable, therefore, that father's actual presence at such a time is of extreme importance—actual, not nominal; it is through and by the emergence of another person that discrimination, possibility of choice, a feeling for conflicting values is established. In other words, the father's presence is needed for a sound development of the ego. When father's otherness can be experienced as a constructive, positive force supplementing mother's, even though at times at variance with her and yet also valid, it is easier for the child to dis-identify from the mother, to establish himself according to his own law, and eventually to form a relationship with a thou. This is a particularly difficult problem for the girl since her first relationship, that with the mother, is a relationship of sameness, and therefore it seems to her as if all relationship is based on identification. For a boy, it is vital that he should be able to project hero-qualities onto his father that enable him to break the tie with mother. There is one other aspect that can play an essential part in the life of a child, namely the role of father as comforter; mother comforts when in pain or distress of body, but it is father who is the comforter when in pain or distress of soul or mind. Father the comforter is also father the provider.

DIFFERENCE BETWEEN THE FUNCTIONS OF MOTHER AND FATHER

Mother is the bearer of new life and the birth-giver: as image she remains forever the world of origin, of timelessness, the womb to which one would return for warmth and security and fulfilment; she is the world that provides food and protection; she is the earth in which one would sleep. Mother's timelessness is nature's rhythm in which birth and death alternate. There is constancy about this rhythm and about this image, irrespective of whether the actual experience of the personal mother was good or bad. Mother represents the unconscious, the instinctive side of life as it has been and always will be on this earth.

There was a time, it has been thought, when the connection between coitus and conception was unknown or not admitted. Then fertilization happened through a spirit, a spirit in the form of man, creature, voice—a presence. Father did not exist, only mother. But never has it been thought that father existed without mother. Rather father came into being during historical time when man's creative forces were recognized as more independent of nature than were woman's.

Father embodies consciousness; his realm is reason and knowledge, light and sun. In a patriarchal society it is the elders, the fathers, who govern, who pass laws and keep tradition alive. For the child it is the father who is the mediator between the exciting world outside and the home. His attitude to work, ambition, success, and competition affects and colors the child's attitude and can make him long to grow up or be afraid to do so. It is the father's strength that provides security and encourages self-confidence, and his authority that helps the child discover his boundaries. This is the way in which the father gives birth to his children.

It is understandable at a time when the father's role has become so problematical that father passes on his insecurity to his children: fatherlessness brings about ego-deficiency. The overemphasis on the role of the mother encourages a false ego that relies on opinions and collective ideas and operates in a kind of gang or pack mentality. The father who is there and yet not there can be much more difficult for the child than a father who believes in himself. When father does not embody authority and security a child's feelings of resentment, aggression, frustration and despair at not being able to project ideals and values onto him may be vented on society and the state.

In an environment in which mother's powers are too seductive, there is the danger of being drawn back into her realm; it is dangerous for the individual to remain too near her values without the compensatory values of the father-world holding the balance: the unconscious overcompensation is the overemphasis on rationality, our twentieth century mind, materialism, our "childish passion for rational enlightenment,"[2] which Jung said was the cause of many neuroses.

In some way, however, mother is becoming more conscious of her potentially dangerous side; man has yet to apply his more developed sense of consciousness to himself as father. At this point, he seems to have little idea of his positive side, but even less of how destructive he can be.

---

2. "The Aims of Psychotherapy," in *CW* 16, §99.

There are different kinds of psychologically absent fathers: one of them is the father "out of work" who does not "provide"; another is the weak father who is despised by his wife secretly or overtly. He may be weak as a character; he may drink, or gamble, or run after women, or he may be inefficient in a general way. His feelings of in-sufficiency, nonentity and insecurity may affect his children in the form of an anxiety neurosis, frigidity, impotence, or in the form of having feelings of being stuck—others can, I can't. Unconscious resentment can make a child's contempt for the father's weakness more bitter.

Then there is the jealous Jehovah-like father who blusters and is angry and hurt if his will is not done or his advice taken on every issue. This may be one of the causes that lead to a compulsion neurosis, and his children may be people who try too hard, who are obsessed with being successful, who tend to overstrain.

In a general way one finds that whenever someone is abject about rules and regulations, or flaunts them automatically, afraid of or has difficulties with external authority, there is a father-complex in the background. This is also true for those who have difficulties with time: fear of time, over-punctual or unable to be punctual.

The over-conservative father can be one of the most dangerous ones for the child. Negative and castrating, such a father inhibits life by resisting change, development, and transformation. In myth the image of this father is Kronos who devoured his children because he did not want them to be in time and space. In the external world he is the father whose ideas are based on the collective conscious attitudes of his father's era, fearing the current ones. He is terrible because he teaches to resist and opposes the new, attempting to fixate consciousness in his way, allowing for no other.

The ego is the carrier of consciousness, of ideals and intentions of life—in time. Whereas mother in her eternal aspect represents the earth that does not change, the transpersonal father represents consciousness as it moves and changes. In this sense father is subject to time, subject to ageing and death; his image changes with the culture he represents. Constancy within change is the secret of the father principle as spirit, his activating, fertilizing, life-giving, creative power coming from another plane, or adding another dimension to the earthly plane.

Change is the dynamic aspect of life in this world, and it is the truly pos-itive father who allows it.

When a girl experiences father in his destructive aspect and fights him, she can lead a relatively undisturbed feminine existence, because she rejects only what is alien to her. Nevertheless, her capacity for sex-ual relationship may be damaged, also her potential for lucidity and objectivity; she may remain stuck in the obscure, ambiguous, uncon-scious level of her nature. Because her ego development is impaired, she will rely on opinions and be rebellious in a collective way, being much more contaminated by her father's collective ideas and attitudes than she knows or can admit.

As is well known, it is the father who is the first to arouse the girl's sexuality with regard to man. The incestuous desires are deeply repressed by the child; but quite as often the father is as unconscious of his desires and of the strength of his feelings for, and jealousy of, his daughter. It depends on his attitude to his feminine side, to his relation-ship with his wife, and to the relationship he had with his mother as to how he will react to his daughter's desires and fears.

His reaction then will influence the girl in her attitude to her emo-tional life and in her relationship to man. When her feelings are ignored or laughed at, she will have feelings of shame and inferiority that go very deep and are difficult to overcome.

When father reacts too strongly, a girl may become frightened of physical contact: father becomes disgusting. She will fear both father's reaction and her own feelings, because they have been made to feel dis-gusting—by mother.

Fantasies and daydreams about an ideal father color ideas about an ideal man who is utterly removed from reality. A result of this mixture of fantasy and repression is that a girl may regress to the level of primi-tive woman so that a "spirit" has to father her child; relationship is nei-ther present nor expected (illegitimacy!); or else in the arms of her hus-band or lover a woman has the child from her "spirit" lover, and then the child is a very special child and particularly beloved.

In this connection, a phenomenon has to be mentioned through which it is possible to learn a great deal about the secret physical and spiritual longings that have to do with the father. I refer to the women, married and unmarried, who fall in love with men who carry the mantle of father: i. e., doctors, analysts, clergymen. Very complicated and tragic situations can arise, though this experience can also be a gateway to new insight, greater consciousness and understanding for the inner meaning of incest.

Reasons for choice of husband are connected with the father; if a woman denies this, it means that she has a father-complex and is unconscious of it. Every little girl expresses a wish to marry a man exactly like or exactly unlike her father. Problems that arise in marriage between the wife and her husband—as far as the wife is concerned—have to do with the unsolved problems between the woman and her father, or even with problems which her parents had been unable to solve between themselves. This is the case when a man turns out to be like father, a drunkard, running after women, or impotent. The problem then is so urgent that it appears "outside," though in fact it has to do with that part within which is father. Unfortunately, even though made conscious, it does not always mean that such problems can be solved within marriage; a marriage may have to break up, which may be the price that has to be paid for greater consciousness (though it is obviously not always greater consciousness that leads to a marriage being broken up).

For the girl, the father is the mediator of the male principle as spirit, as well as of the masculine sex; as spirit he represents the essentially other. The actual experience of the personal father may be helpful and give confidence in undertaking marriage as a means for creating a union in the external world, and also a desire eventually to go on the inner quest that may bring about an experience of one's totality and essence. Or the actual experience with father may have been disastrous, and then an outer relationship may not have come about or succeeded, but still the inner way, however difficult, may prove fruitful in bringing to consciousness a sense of meaning and purpose into a life in which the spirit of man was hidden behind a flaming Jehovah, or else, even worse, into a life in which there was not even an anger to encounter—just nothingness and a void.

Father's relationship to the son has particular characteristics: through Jung's Association Experiment it is known that typologically the son is closer to his father than to his mother. "Alikeness" may create difficulties in any relationship, all the more in the one to the father, particularly if the father recognizes his shadow side in the son, or the other way round, the son in his parent.

In our society the son's fear of the father is largely due to the Oedipal situation and the well-known conflict that accompanies it. The incest wish in the boy differs from that of the girl's: he wants to be with mother, inside her, alone, without father, warm and safe. But he does not think in terms of having a child from her as does the girl with regard to her father. For the boy the sexual act does not mean the creation of new life, but it is copulation and a way to prove his virility and his ability to compete with his father. This is where one meets the boy's ambivalence: his envy of his father's great power also means that he admires his father; furthermore, he may feel a certain tenderness for the father who possesses mother. Real difficulties arise when mother is "too welcoming," giving the impression that her son is more important to her than her husband, or else if she is too rejecting of the son's feelings. Problems arise too if the boy feels that his father treats him in a too humiliating fashion. Then the boy may find himself in a no man's land of no existence, and can only escape by going into fantasy—into masturbatory fantasies in which he is omnipotent, and which cut him off from outer reality and relationship.

Fantasy may prevent the boy from fighting his father—he may be too afraid, or too removed from reality; but he may still remain utterly dependent on the personal father's approval and acceptance. Castrated, he either loses the connection to his own creative powers, to the transpersonal father-creator in himself, or else he flees into identification with the father-god as Holy Spirit and remains in a possessed state of heavenly inflation. Both these states signify that the ego has missed out; too much fear has maimed the spirit of aggression.

An early conflict with the father on the emotional plane in which he appears either as a hostile or despicable figure is not the only level on which the father-dragon has to be overcome.

The father-son conflict typifies the great problem of all time, the problem between the generations; it is not always recognized in all its poignancy, for the Oedipal situation is only one aspect of it. Rivalry between father and son is different in kind from rivalry between equals; a very particular helplessness is experienced by the child who is in the power of the father, and by the father who is in the power of time. Mythologically, this conflict is expressed in the stories of the ageing gods and the fights between the old and the young. Historically the problem was acted out by royal persons governing the community: the old king fought to retain his power; the young king designate attempted to wrest the realm from him. It is only in comparatively late patriarchal civilizations that this controversy between old and young came to be associated with father and son. Erich Neumann contends that the essential motive for the son's hostility against the father is contained in the problem of generations, and is the son's need to find his own validity. The young hero has to fight the old outmoded world of yesterday in order to establish his own inner law and to discover the values of today. The collective law as represented by the father has to be fought by the son with all the misery of fear of punishment, temporal and eternal, which is attached to this rebellion, in order to progress from the traditional moral code to the discovery of conscience.

The idea of hostility to and impatience with yesterday's values and sufferings is a familiar one and runs like a red thread through history. The father's enmity and fear is son can be deduced from the extent of the custom of infanticide, which was practiced almost universally among all peoples, and certainly among the Assyrians, Babylonians, Jews—and from the practice of exposing children, as among the Indians and the Greeks. The firstborn son, in particular, carried the father's ambivalence of feeling, and was sacrificed in order to appease an angry god. The angry god, then as now, is the father's anger at the new life that will supplant him, and the fear of death. The killing, however, is also a sacrifice, because there is not only hate for the son, but love too, and the idea of life being continued through him.

The conflict between an individual father and son can be resolved when both recognize the angry jealous God in themselves, and when they are able to differentiate between the actual person, be it father, be it son, and the fantasy image born from projections, wishful thinking and archetypal ideas. Only too frequently do fathers and sons believe that their terrible relationship, their emotional difficulties are purely personal; whereas this conflict is a collective one that concerns every father and son.

In various religions, the father-son relationship is at the center. In Jewish and Christian thought it is so on a personal level, as well as depicting the relationship between God and man. In a parallel way, the image of the father-son relationship is used in Indian philosophy as describing the relationship between true self and ego.

For the Vedantic Indian, the physical father and the whole domain of the physical senses, organs of reason, as well as inherited customs and prejudices of one's race must be put aside before one can enter into the full possession of one's intrinsic self.

The ideas link up with alchemy in which the problem of "generations" is expressed as the rejuvenation, transformation and rebirth of the father, the old man or the old king who is ill, sometimes evil and petrified, who has to die; by dissolving in water or in the mother's womb he can be reborn, renewed as the son or the young king. By implication, the alchemists drew a parallel between the old king and the young king, on the one hand, and God and his son, on the other—an indication that God as Father needs to be reborn.

Jung doubted that the alchemists were conscious of this implication. I believe they probably were, for in the daily living of the liturgy and in the concept of the Trinity the pain of constant transformation is expressed: the need for sacrifice, the willingness to be sacrificed and the spirit by which this is accomplished, always anew the sacrifice of the yesterday—the yesterday we hold so dear.

There is one religion, Islam, which does not tolerate the term "father" in reference to God. Muslims understood the word "father" only in the sense of physical generation, which means that if God is father he must have a wife. And so they will not even admit the term in the metaphysical sense of God as the father of man.

The reconciliation between the generations is not only an outer problem, but essentially an inner one. From the child's point of view, reconciliation is ultimately the coming to terms with the internalized inner parent image; from the father's, it is the coming to terms with his child, the outer and the inner too. The first step is to recognize that there is an inner fantasy image, and not exclusively an outer reality. The unhappy child within, in parent and child, has to look at the expectations and the disappointments, at the contentments, at the envy and greed as well as at the gratitude and generosity in himself. These feelings have to be permitted and, if possible, understood. All these emotions have to do with the earliest time of life, with mother, and it is often arduous to get at these experiences in analysis. But there is a level on which we are deeply influenced by the father and of which we may remain unconscious much longer than of any emotional disturbances experienced at the breast. It is a level that is unconscious but not repressed; it is the level on which father is an appendix of mother, in relationship to mother, unknown, vague, known only through and by mother. And yet he is there; his attitude of thought, his behavior, his spirituality are conveyed indirectly, and subliminally experienced. All these attitudes form part of the internalized father image, and we may remain unconscious for a long time to what an extent we are identified with and conditioned by this image. Even a dawning of this situation heralds a new phase: it means that we are separating the inner parent figures, that we can experience the importance and the validity of both parents, that we are withdrawing projections. With the ego thus strengthened there will be less neurotic conflict, the inner parent images can join in a new deliberate union, and can give birth to self.

BIBLIOGRAPHY

Adler, Gerhard. *The Living Symbol: A Case Study in the Process of Individuation* (New York: Pantheon Books, 1961)

Allenby, Amy I. "The Father Archetype in Feminine Psychology," *The Journal of Analytical Psychology* 1, no. 1 (1955)

Bitter, Wilhelm, ed. *Vorträge über das Vaterproblem in Psychotherapie, Religion und Gesellschaft* (Stuttgart: Hippokrates Verlag, 1954)

Fordham, Michael. *The Life of Childhood: A Contribution to Analytical Psychology* (London: Kegan Paul, Trench, Trubner & Co., 1944)

Jung, C. G. (1949). *The Significance of the Father in the Destiny of the Individual*, in *CW* 4

—. *The Archetypes and the Collective Unconscious*, in *CW* 9.1

—. *The Development of Personality*, in *CW* 17

—. *Mysterium Coniunctionis*, in *CW* 14

Neumann, Erich. *The Origins and History of Consciousness* (New York: Pantheon, 1954)

Social Casework (January and October 1954; April 1957)

www.ingramcontent.com/pod-product-compliance
Lightning Source LLC
Chambersburg PA
CBHW020252290326
41930CB00039B/742